Dvořák

Dvořák

Kurt Honolka

translated by Anne Wyburd

HAUS PUBLISHING · LONDON

First published in German in the Rowohlt monographien 1974
series © 2000 Rowohlt Taschenbuch Verlag GmbH

This English translation first published in Great Britain
in 2004 by Haus Publishing Limited
26 Cadogan Court
Draycott Avenue
London
SW3 3BX

English translation© Anne Wyburd, 2004

The moral right of the author has been asserted

A CIP catalogue record for this book is available from the British Library

ISBN 1-904341-52-7

Typeset by Lobster Design
Printed and bound by Graphicom in Vicenza, Italy

Cover image: Courtesy Topham Picturepoint
Back cover: Courtesy Lebrecht Picture Library

Contents

Dvořák

Janáček

Smetana

The Creators of Czech National Music

Smetana and Dvořák – to a certain extent the musical world pronounces these two great names in one breath, as undisputedly the most outstanding representatives of Czech music, who occupy an assured place in the 'classical' category of world music. As a result of a remarkable posthumous renaissance, a third name – Janáček – has recently joined them and his oeuvre as an opera composer complements both his predecessors on an international level, though this in no way diminishes their fame as pioneers, especially among their compatriots.

Bedřich Smetana (1824–1884) is regarded as the founder of the Czech national school of composition. His Op 1 was dedicated to Franz Liszt, who arranged for its publication. His orchestral masterpieces, the six pieces that make up *Má Vlast*, were composed over five years from 1874–9. In 1876 he composed the extraordinarily confessional 2nd Quartet *Z mého života (From My Life)*, documenting his descent into deafness with a candour that would not be surpassed in the Czech tradition until the Janáček string quartets. His death in 1884 resulted in a genuine national grief.

In the last quarter of the 20th century Janáček's unconventional operas like *The Macropoulos Case* or *From the House of the Dead* may have come to seem more interesting to the Germans and to the English than Smetana's eight operas and Dvořák's ten put together, while his two string quartets (rated as 'new music') are possibly more intriguing than Dvořák's incomparably larger output of chamber music. These are value judgements made from the historical and developmental perspectives of today and say little about the historical standing of the older founding fathers.

Bedřich Smetana holds the honorary title of 'Creator of Czech national music', which is certainly as much deserved as Glinka's title of 'Father of Russian music', however poetically transcendental such epithets may tend to be. Smetana gave his nation the first truly Czech opera, *The Brandenburgers in Bohemia (Branboři v Čechách)*, and the same year, 1866, also saw the premiere of the most widely performed Czech opera ever – *The Bartered Bride (Prodaná nevěsta)*. To them he added a patriotic musical apotheosis of a national homeland and history, the symphonic cycle *Má Vlast (My Fatherland)*. However, he wrote little chamber music, no symphonies and no oratorios, and his compatriot Antonín Dvořák, 17 years his junior, was his equal and complementary partner in these fields of composition.

Bracketing together Smetana and Dvořák – reminiscent of 'Goethe and Schiller' as personifications of a golden age – is not the only example in the cultural history of Czech national identity. It has its parallels in 19th-century literature as well (the poet Karel Hynek Mácha and the author Božena Němcová) and in painting (the joint founders being Josef Mánes and Mikoláš Aleš). However, although Smetana and Dvořák are internationally acknowledged as the exclusive representatives of this musical rebirth, this is not so unequivocally endorsed from the Czech historical standpoint. At the end of the 19th century Czech musicology regarded the creators of their national music not as a duo but a trio, including the name of Zdeněk Fibich and placing him and Dvořák on the same level but below Smetana. In 1966 a leading modern Czech composer, Jarmil Burghauser, wrote a book which lauded Smetana, Dvořák and Fibich as a mutually complementary constellation of Czech national composers.[1] No one outside Czechoslovakia knows Fibich except as the originator of a piece of light music called *Poem*, but to the Czechs this highly versatile musician also ranks as one of their classic composers. His melodrama trilogy *Hippodamia* is an original composition, though limited by its parochial character.

The discrepancy between national and international reputation is also reflected in the esteem accorded to Smetana and Dvořák. The music of the latter is played much more often in concert halls worldwide than is that of the former in opera houses where, apart from some sporadic revivals, only *The Bartered Bride* is generally known. At home, though he is very popular, Dvořák is ranked well behind Smetana, whose chronological precedence is further enhanced by the overwhelmingly important role in the national and cultural renaissance accorded to Czech opera – which he founded and which Dvořák only enriched without surpassing him – as well as by his eminent interpreters. In

Zdeněk Fibich, (1850–1900) studied piano with Moscheles and composition with Lachner in Mannheim. He was conductor at the Provisional Theatre 1875–8. He was equally influenced by the opposing compositional aesthetics of both Schumann and Wagner. He was director of the Russian Orthodox Church choir from 1878–81 His operas, especially *The Fall of Arkun* and *The Bride of Messina* are central to the Czech canon, though much of the rest of his enormous output (over 700 works) is generally unknown.

the face of authorities like Otakar Hostinský, the founder of modern Czech musical aesthetics, and Smetana's biographer Zdeněk Nejedlý, who in his last years as Culture Minister in Communist Czechoslovakia wielded an overwhelming political influence on the arts to the detriment of Dvořák, Dvořák's admirers were at a considerable disadvantage, even though the musicologist Otakar Šourek produced a comprehensive four-volume monograph on Dvořák, while Nejedlý's projected standard work on Smetana remained unfinished.

Czech national music is a latecomer to Europe. Glinka (1804–1857), the father of Russian music, was a generation older than Smetana, and even Chopin and Moniuszko in Poland preceded him. That the Czechs lagged behind seems surprising when one remembers how for centuries Czech classical music had been closely connected with the stylistically pioneering West, above all

Waldstein's Palace in Prague by
Josef Setelika

of course with its German neighbours, and how rich its own contribution had been for a long time. In the 9th century, during the brief period of the independent Great Moravian Empire, masses were already being sung not in Latin but in Old Slav. The oldest musical manuscripts in Bohemia go back to the 11th century; there were troubadours at the Přemyslid court in Prague, and the influence of medieval German tradition was enriched by French polyphony and the Italian early Renaissance, particularly during the reign of Charles IV of Luxembourg who was a patron of the arts. In the form of the Hussite chorale, which bestowed a radiance on the later chorales of the Lutheran Reformation, Czech Bohemia gave back what it had for centuries been receiving from the example and inspiration of German culture. Through the abundance of so-called 'minor masters' who had emigrated in the baroque period, Bohemia and Moravia made a vital contribution to European classicism. Charles Burney, who travelled widely in Europe, bore witness to the flourishing musical life of Bohemia, on the basis of which it became known as the 'Conservatory of Europe'.

Among many others, George (Jiří) Benda, who emigrated like so many musicians whose country could no longer support them, created the art form of the melodrama; Johann Stamitz founded the historically important Mannheim School; Antonín Rejcha was an important influence on Beethoven and both Czechs and Germans from Bohemia and Moravia contributed to this musical renown. Czech nationalistic feeling for musical history – if anything intensified under Communism – tried to annex artists for the Czech nation. Stamitz, for instance, was given Czech nationality, though the musicologist Peter Gradenwitz (now an Israeli)[2] had already proved in 1936 that he was of Austro-German origin, quite apart from the fact that he then took up residence in Mannheim. Nationalism was completely alien to musicians of the 18th century, when to be a Bohemian meant that you came from Bohemia, whatever your mother tongue might be, but in the second half of the 19th century, when the paths of the two peoples living in Bohemia began to diverge, Czech and German Bohemians were referred to separately in German. Not so in Czech, for the word 'Český' meant both a resident of Bohemia and a Czech citizen. This linguistic distinction drew Czech historical writing retrospectively towards a kind of cultural–political imperialism which is historically incorrect but which, together with its emphatically anti-German feeling, can be explained by the defensiveness of a populace which for centuries had had to fight for its basic existence as a nation.

The Thirty Years War was not just an economic disaster for the Czechs, but a national and cultural one as well. After the battle of the White Mountain near Prague in 1620 they lost the independence which they had maintained throughout the Middle Ages within the loose federation of the Holy Roman Empire of German nations. Now they were to be ruled no longer by their own princes but by the Habsburgs in Vienna, whose Counter-Reformation policy in Bohemia and Moravia was motivated not by nationalism but rather by religious and dynastic politics. In the event, as both regions were almost entirely Protestant, the result of this policy was to destroy the Czechs. There was mass confiscation of Protestant-owned property, a new nobility was

The Charles Bridge over the river Vltava in Prague by Josef Setelika

created out of foreign settlers loyal to the Habsburgs (Colloredo, Schwarzenberg, Clam-Galls, Buquoy and Piccolomini), citizens' rights were suppressed in favour of a growing, centralised bureaucracy and with them went the development of the Czech language. Many Czechs unwilling to become Catholics emigrated, among them the great pedagogue Johann Amos Comenius (Jan Amos Komenský); predominantly Catholic Germans settled in the border areas devastated by the war. The peasants sank into serfdom and German became increasingly the language of culture in the towns. Czech schools, let alone universities, did not exist in the first half of the 19th century, Czech literature withered into insignificance in the provinces and the Czech language only survived among the social underclass in the towns and the peasantry in the country.

It is therefore understandable that these 'baroque' centuries, when the building activities of the nobility and the Jesuits were defining the character of the principal city of Prague and of count-less towns and villages, were regarded by the Czechs as the Dark Ages. So far as music was concerned, folk song and village music-making flourished, and in the field of serious music, whose patrons were the nobility and the church, the country produced abundant talent – more, in fact, than it could support. This famous Bohemian musicianship (which also included the German Bohemians) could not, however, create a definite character for itself, for it had no formative stylistic centre. The first so-called 'National Theatre' in Prague, founded in 1783 by Count Nostitz, a member of the old Bohemian aristocracy, was famous for stag-ing the world premiere of Mozart's *Don Giovanni*. It still stands today close to the Charles University but it was expressly oriented towards German ideals. The people, according to the intention of the Count's dedication, were to promote 'the works of German masters in German to a worthy standard and in a worthy setting'.

At that time even the Czechs could only grasp the concept of 'Bohemian' as a symbiosis of German–Czech culture. The first Czech-language operetta – Joseph Weigl's *Schweizerfamilie (Swiss Family)* – only appeared in 1823, followed three years later by the first by a Czech composer, *Dráteník (The Tinker)* by František Škroup, but this was completely Austro-German in style, as were his other stage works. Even the style of the song *Kde domov můj* from Škroup's operetta *Fidlovačka (The Shoemakers' Festival)*, which was adopted as the official national anthem of the Czechoslovak Republic, is less typically Czech than German in the romantic style of the time. Even Smetana, who was perforce educated in German schools and only learnt to write Czech well in his old age, found nothing strange in basing his patriotic operas *Dalibor* and *Libuše* on German libretti by the Austrian Adolf Wenzig.

By the time Smetana wrote the first truly Czech opera, the process of his people's national and cultural rebirth was already well under way, springing from an endangered basis – the Czech language. Herder's rediscovery of the treasures of European folk poetry *Stimmen der Völker in Liedern* (*Voices of the People in Songs*) exerted a powerful influence on Bohemia and his heightened regard for the 'gentle Slav' strengthened self-awareness in the Czech soul. Around 1800 Josef Dobrovský set down (in German) the ground-rules for teaching modern Czech and founded Czech Slavistics, while Josef Jungmann researched and codified the treasures of the Czech language, hitherto despised by the educated classes. Poets such as the romantic Karel Hynek Mácha, who died young, Jan Kollár, František Ladislav Čelakovský and Josef Kajetán Tyl enriched the language with their poetry, novels and plays and the historian František Palacký awakened pride in his nation's happier, glorious past – a pride which had enjoyed a brief flowering in 1817. The student Václav Hanka, depressed that no documents on the old Czech heroic sagas were available, published sophisticated 'medieval' manuscripts to the enthusiasm of generations of Czechs, until Tomáš Garrigue Masaryk's undisputed scholarship finally unmasked them as forgeries.

Stronger than the ideas of the 'Grande Révolution', quelled by the Metternich regime, was the spark of nationalist feeling kindled by the Germans in the breasts of the Czechs during the Napoleonic era, in the spirit of which Miroslav Tyrš founded the Bohemian Gymnastic Society called Sokol (The Hawk) on the model created in 1811 by the German Friedrich Jahn, the so-called 'father of gymnastics'. Even in the politics of culture the Czech revival of pre-1848 days mainly took its bearings from German intellectual movements: in philosophy from Kant and Hegel, in literature from Goethe, Schiller and the romantics, in music initially from Mozart and Beethoven and later from the 'new Germans' Wagner and Liszt, not forgetting the inspiring example of the folk operas by Carl Maria von Weber, who spent several years as conductor at Nostitz's National Theatre in Prague.

In the first half of the 19th century a wave of national enthusiasm flowed through the Czech middle classes, awakened and strengthened by the economic developments of burgeoning industrialisation, which challenged the autocratic rule exerted over their property by the country nobility, and by the need to catch up on two centuries of 'darkness'. People in the towns began to found associations, musical societies and academies to promote public concerts. Before the antagonistic rift between Czechs and Germans in Bohemia – at least until the revolution of 1848/9 – this Czech revival continued under the name of Bohemianism without any chauvinistic overtone.

THE GREAT BARRICADE IN THE BREITEN-STRASSE, BERLIN.—(SEE PAGE 214.)

Revolution in Berlin, 1848 Barricade on the Breiten-Strasse

Apart from the Czechs themselves, the German Bohemian Karl Egon Ebert and the Austrian Franz Grillparzer, who sang the praises of Libussa (Libuše), also enthused over the glories of Bohemia's heroic past. In pre-1848 Czech music neither the composer Škroup nor Pavel Křížkovský, a prolific writer of Czech choruses, showed any nationalistic or even original national traits.

This was the situation which, in spite of their difference in age, Dvořák and Smetana came into almost simultaneously, when around the middle of the century they both began working in Prague. It is essential to know about these preconditions if one is to understand why these musically highly talented Czechs with powerfully individual voices came so late onto the international musical scene, and to appreciate how high creative genius had to rise above mediocre circumstances if it was to fulfil its mission.

Youth and Student Years 1841–1859

A creative artist's birthplace need not necessarily be of vital significance in his life. What has Gluck to do with the Upper Palatinate or Beethoven with the Rhineland? In Dvořák's case, however, the landscape of his childhood undoubtedly affected his destiny. Czech sagas venerate two mountains as holy. The Vyšehrad, at the southern gateway to Prague, drops down steeply to the Vltava (there is a road tunnel under it today) and was in ancient times known as the seat of Libussa, the legendary original ruler of the city. In the cemetery above lie many famous Czechs, among them Smetana (who immortalised the mountain in *Má Vlast*) and also Dvořák. Seventy kilometres to the north as the

Woodcut of Nelahozeves, the palace of the Lobkovitz princes in the background

crow flies the solitary outcrop of the Řip, or George Mountain, towers over the gently sloping plain of Central Bohemia. From its peaks in ancient times Čech, the father of his people, coming from the east at the head of his tribe, is said to have looked down on their new homeland and decided that this was a 'good place to be'. More or less halfway between them, about 30 kilometres north of Prague and also on the Vltava, lies Nelahozeves, the village where Dvořák was born and which, being at the time in bilingual Eastern Austria, was also called Mühlhausen.

The village on the banks of the river is dominated by the huge, four-square, towering Renaissance palace of the Lobkovitz princes, below which lie a Gothic parish church and simple labourers' houses, number 12 being one of the finest. It consisted of a dwelling-house with a single-storey shop connected to it by an archway and there Antonín Dvořák was born on 8 September 1841. The Vltava flowing past on one side is not an imposing river but a narrow, sluggish stream with little traffic on it, and all around stretches a flat landscape of copses, orchards and fields of golden grain – not exciting or heroic but very homely and friendly, long fertile and civilised, the villages close together,

inviting neighbourliness. Dvořák loved it. Here he grew up and in his middle years, when he was in a position to choose a country property, came back to the Southern Bohemian village of Vysoká. Unlike Smetana, the intellectual townsman, who was only driven into the provinces by the misfortune of his deafness, Dvořák, while choosing to live in Prague, remained a countryman at heart and even when he was living in New York he always rose early.

Dvořák's birthplace at Nelahozeves

Antonín was the eldest of nine children born to the innkeeper and butcher František Dvořák (1814–1894) and his wife Anna, née Zdeňková. For generations the Dvořáks had been innkeepers and butchers in the area – trades which went well together – but a whiff of higher social class crept in from his mother's side, her father having worked as a bailiff for Prince Lobkovitz. However, we do not know what legacy she left her famous son, for not even a faded picture of her survives. Old photos show that, like Goethe, he had inherited his physiognomy from his father, who had a broad, typically Slav face with deep-set dark eyes under bushy eyebrows. He also inherited some of his nature: father Dvořák was a very practical, peasant type and far from unmusical. He was an accomplished zither player and in later years even earned some much-needed extra money from his playing, while two of his brothers were well known for their skill on the fiddle and the trumpet. Making music was in the Dvořák family's blood.

At home little Antonín was called Anton (the German form of his name), which indicates that at the time simple Czech people had no sense of nationalism. He grew up surrounded by local folk music and the songs he heard in those days had not been refined but were passed as living entities from mouth to mouth. People sang in church choirs and played for dancing in the inns, where Antonín the schoolboy joined in on the fiddle which he learnt to play at an early age from Joseph Spitz, his teacher at the single-class Czech primary school.[3] Spitz was a good musician and according to his daughter could 'play every instrument'. Father Dvořák was pleased about his eldest son's musical gifts and encouraged them but without ever thinking of letting him become a professional musician. On the contrary, at the age of 13 he sent him to the neighbouring small town of Zlonice for two practical reasons: to learn proper German and the butcher's trade.

For the next two years Antonín lived with his uncle, working as an apprentice butcher and graduating to be a journeyman (without a doubt the only great composer in musical history to have trained as a butcher), but the years in Zlonice, which he commemorated later in his first symphony which he called *The Bells of Zlonice (Zlonické zvony)*, decisively influenced his future career for quite another reason: at the German secondary school his language teacher Anton Liehmann, who came from German North Bohemia, greatly encouraged his musical talents. Liehmann played a number of instruments including the organ, on which he performed superbly in Viennese classical style in the lovely late-baroque Dientzenhofer church, and he also composed music for his amateur orchestra. He taught Antonín to play the organ, the piano and the viola, instructed him in music theory and introduced him for the first time to the great composers, especially Beethoven. His most famous pupil remembered him as *a good musician, but short-tempered. He still taught by the old methods: if you couldn't play something you got as many punches in the ribs as there*

'The Great Inn' in Zlonice, home to the Dvořák family from 1854

were notes on the page.[4] Rather than resenting this autocratic teaching method, Dvořák was frankly grateful to him. In the person of the cantor Benda in his opera *The Jacobin* (*Jakobín*), whose daughter he called Terynka after Liehmann's daughter, he paid a loving tribute to his strict teacher and to all the little village cantors who within living memory had through their diligent, practical music-making ensured that Bohemia became the 'conservatory of Europe'. It is an irony for national chauvinism that the real-life model for the 'Czech' (or in other words 'Bohemian') cantor immortalised here by Dvořák was a man of German origin.

For Dvořák himself this was no problem; from Liehmann he learnt German and music – the latter admittedly much better than the former, so that his father, who had meanwhile moved with the family to Zlonice, sent him away again, this time for the express purpose of learning German, to the little town of Böhmisch-Kamnitz (Česke Kamenice) in wholly German-speaking North Bohemia. He exchanged places for a year with a miller's son, who went to live with the Dvořáks – a sensible arrangement which was still being practised in Bohemia a century later. Dvořák liked living among the German Bohemians, attended the German school and found a second Liehmann[5] in Franz Hanke, the choirmaster of the Deanery Church, who continued his training on the organ and in musical theory and gave him sympathetic encouragement.

On Dvořák's return home there arose the question of his future career. His father insisted on his becoming a master-butcher while Liehmann and his uncle Zdeněk urged him to let his son develop his promising musical talent professionally in Prague. (He had already composed a few pieces, including a Franz-Joseph March.) His father finally gave way but insisted that if he was to become a musician he must take up a solid, practical career as an organist. So the 16-year old travelled to Prague on a peasant's wagon (cheaper than the railway), happy that he would not have to

The rooftops of Prague, painting by Josef Setelika

become an innkeeper and cut up meat, and full of hopes and expectations.

Prague in 1857 in no way corresponded to today's idea of a metropolis. Capital of Bohemia, an architectural jewel with its gothic towers and baroque palaces, it lay completely in the shadow of the imperial city of Vienna with which it was not yet even connected by the railway. It was an old-fashioned provincial town, where Jews still lived in a ghetto, where most of the populace – merchants, officials and educated people – only spoke German, where the beginnings of industrialisation strengthened the Czech element only in the suburbs and where all the upper schools still taught in German. The conciliatory move towards 'Bohemianism' had received a mortal blow in the brutal suppression of the 1848/9 revolution by the Habsburg General Windischgrätz. Opinions were already divided at the German National Assembly in Frankfurt, for the Czechs were pinning their hopes not just on German democracy but on the renewal of Bohemian constitutional law within the framework of a Habsburg federal state. They considered they had been let down by the suppression of the revolution and began to go their own way. Statements like that of the influential Graf Thun, a descendant of the old aristocratic family which had led the Protestant anti-Habsburg party in the Thirty Years War – 'I am neither German nor Czech; I am a Bohemian!' – had become even more anachronistic after the upheaval of 1848/9. This nationalistic ferment bothered young Dvořák no more than the fact that lessons at the Organ School in the ancient Arkadenhof in the Konviktgasse (now Konvitská) were conducted in German. He just wanted to become a good musician.

The Organ School had long enjoyed a reputation as the central training place for church musicians. Dvořák attended it for two years, as well as the German training college in the Franciscan Monastery of Maria Schnee. His first director was Karl Franz Pitsch, a German, and after his death Josef Krejčí, a Czech who, strangely enough but significantly in this context, increasingly favoured German-speaking pupils, as emerged in Dvořák's final report: 'Excellent but mostly practical talent. Practical knowledge and ability seem to be his sole objective; he does less well in theory . . . ', to which Dvořák's inadequate knowledge of German had certainly contributed. However he learnt to play the organ competently, was well trained in thorough bass and harmony and had deepened his knowledge of the classical composers Bach, Handel and Beethoven.

Dvořák first stayed with the large family of a relative, master-tailor Jan Plíva, and later with his uncle Václav Dušek. These were years of grinding poverty. He had no piano of his own but his friend Karel Bendl, who came from a well-to-do family, helped him out and he widened his knowledge of musical literature as violist in the orchestra of the German St Cecilia Society, whose conductor Anton Apt did not confine himself to the traditional Prague Mozart-worship. Through him young Dvořák encountered the works of the German romantics Liszt and Wagner and became a lifelong admirer of Schubert who, together with Beethoven, was the inspiration behind his symphonic writing, though his own attempts at composition – copybook fugues and polkas for the piano – do not yet convey that impression. Altogether Dvořák looked back on those years of professional study with very mixed feelings. 'Seemingly for him the Organ School was more a means of qualifying for the formal title of musician than the path leading towards becoming a professional composer. He never actually undervalued the solid theoretical training which he received at the Organ School, but he aimed for greater musical recognition outside it', wrote his friend Josef Zubatý.[6]

In 1859 Dvořák came second in the final examinations. He had finished his training as a musician and now he had to earn his living as such. For some time he had not been able to rely on support from his family, for his father had got into business difficulties and moved to Kladno where things were going no better. Dvořák hoped to obtain a modest position as organist at one of the many Prague churches, but without success. Nevertheless, he remained in Prague. His resolve stood firm; he was determined to make good as a musician. His career dovetailed strangely with that of Smetana, for just as Dvořák first arrived in Prague as a student, Smetana the virtuoso and conductor was leaving the city for Gothenburg. When he returned five years later to give future Czech musical life its decisive impetus, Dvořák had just set down on paper his op 1 and op 2 and started on his career as a composer – secretly, without anyone knowing.

Storm and Stress 1859–1873

Though young Antonín was musically talented, he was no child prodigy. In his youth he had been thoroughly trained and was already brimming over with ideas, secure in his craft, an extraordinarily fast writer and greatly inspired by the flourishing Czech musical life of the 1860s, but as a composer success did not come quickly to him and in fact he reached maturity amazingly late. Twelve years were to pass between his finishing his studies at the Organ School and becoming publicly known as a composer, and another two before he celebrated his first success. However, during those years he had covered hundreds of pages of manuscript paper with scrupulously tidy music, including excessively long symphonies and operas, many of which he burned. He was certainly not what is called an intellectual musician but an indisputably honest and self-critical composer; besides, his output was so lavish that he could afford to put a match to scores he did not approve of any more.

During those twelve years – a period outwardly of grinding poverty and inwardly of storm and stress – his personality was being formed, seemingly by chance. As he could not find a post as a paid organist, he joined the little private orchestra of the conductor Karel Komzák as a violist, playing waltzes, polkas, marches and *potpourris* in restaurants. At the beginning of the 1860s the orchestra was engaged at the Provisional Theatre and Dvořák became its first viola (out of two; there were only 34 players, so they could not perform operas). His annual salary never rose above 348 guilders, too little for even a modest living. Smetana, who was conductor at the Provisional Theatre from 1866, earned 1200 to 2000 guilders and even that was no princely sum. Dvořák needed to supplement his earnings as a private piano teacher and substitute organist, nevertheless, after eleven years he gave up his wretched basic income as a violist and

contented himself with the even more wretched 138 guilders which he earned as organist at the church of St Adalbert. Thereby he won his freedom from orchestral duties and leisure for composition.

One cannot emphasise enough how glaring was the discrepancy between outward poverty and inner enrichment in these twelve years of Dvořák's life. What kind of man was he? A photograph from 1865 shows him at 24 as a handsome young man with a well-trimmed moustache but

Dvořák at 24 in 1865

as yet no beard. He was above average height at over 5' 11", powerfully built, with lively dark brown eyes. He was taciturn and reserved but could get very spirited on the subject of music. As one of his fellow students recalled: 'Dvořák was hot-blooded, short-tempered and impatient and when colleagues teased him he avoided them . . . He was too poor to own a piano and every Saturday he went to the Kváčas' house to play, which did not please Mrs Kváča much, because he always dirtied her newly washed floor. He then rented apartments where there was a piano but again often abused this privilege. For instance, he would get up in the night when an idea came to him and play it through before he forgot it, regardless of the fact that the other occupants of the house were sleeping. As a result he often had to move home. Even when he was living with Anger he often monopolised his piano all day.'[7] Dvořák briefly shared a student flat in the Senovážné náměstí with Mořic Anger (who later became conductor at the Provisional Theatre) and three other musicians. He moved out of his cousin Dušek's apartment because of the children's noise but later moved back again. We know something of his lifestyle from his cousin Anna: 'Antonín had breakfast with us but went to a hostelry for lunch and dinner. He had hired a piano from his tailor for two florins a month; opposite it stood a table and behind that his bed. He often composed in bed as soon as he woke and played through his new idea straight away on the coverlet. If he wrote at the table he held his pen between his teeth and played the piano on his coat or his legs . . . My parents were religious and prayed night and morning on their knees. My mother asked young Dvořák to kneel for his daily prayers. *"Aunt, I pray best over there at the window, looking out at the greenery and the sky!"* I never heard my cousin talk coarsely, frivolously or suggestively. He was thoroughly upright, well behaved and faultless. He never came in late and had no girl-friends or amorous adventures. In the family we used to say that he was afraid of women.'[8]

Josefina and Anna Čermáková, Anna (sitting) became Dvořák's wife

She was wrong! Dvořák certainly talked as little about his love life as he did about anything personal, but we have evidence of at least two amorous episodes. He turned for consolation to Aninka Matějka, the daughter of a colleague in the orchestra, when disappointed in his courtship of the 16-year old Josefina Čermáková, a talented soprano at the Provisional Theatre, whom he met through teaching her the piano and adored with a passion which he kept within the bounds of his Catholic principles. However, his love was not reciprocated and she chose Count Kaunitz (Kounic) in preference to the impecunious musician. Like Mozart, Dvořák consoled himself with her younger sister. Anna (1854–1931), who was also his pupil, had a good contralto voice and in 1873 became his wife. Their first child was born five months after the wedding. For over 30 years Anna shared his life as a faithful and loving partner.

So the years in which the composer grew to maturity seemed unsensational and respectable on the surface but were filled with rich and exciting intellectual events. The 1860s were the heroic decade of Czech renaissance, with the 1866 world premiere of Smetana's *The Bartered Bride* marking the central point of creativity, for even though it was initially a failure, it was soon acknowledged as a jewel in the national crown. Important political and cultural developments had taken place. The Habsburg defeat in the Italian campaign at the battle of Solferino in 1859 had its effect on the Czechs: absolutism and censorship had to be relaxed and a law which gave partial freedom to the press resulted in the inauguration of Czech newspapers, among them the *Národní listy*, which for decades was the standard mouthpiece of the middle classes with Smetana as music editor, and *Dalibor,* the groundbreaking progressive musical journal which supported Smetana's reforms. This was the moment for founding new organisations: in 1861 the Choral Society Hlahol (still in existence today), and soon after the nationalistic gymnastic society Sokol and the Artistic Association (Umělecká beseda) for promoting concerts. In 1862 the Czechs moved out of the traditional German Ständetheater, where they had only been temporarily tolerated, and into the newly built Provisional Theatre (Prozatímní divadlo) on the Vltava Embankment.

The Provisional Theatre was not far from the National Theatre and was long ago torn down, as were the other two theatres built at that time – the Neustädter Theater and the New Czech Theatre on the other side of the Korntor (now Žitná), both scenes of historic Smetana premieres. In the narrow orchestra pit of the Provisional Theatre Dvořák played his viola and took part in landmark performances in the birth of Czech opera. To have their own theatre was at that time not just an incidental amenity for the townsfolk – it was a matter of national importance. In 1850 a committee had been formed and the following declaration was made: 'A Czech theatre is what our nation needs . . . Such a temple to [the muse] Thalia, where life appears before our eyes in all its light and shadow, where human foolishness is castigated with unmerciful scorn and distinguished from the truth, where the victory of truth and justice ever bears witness to a higher power, where at last history with all its great figures appears in its full glory as the teacher of mankind.'[9] Building the Provisional Theatre did not yet achieve this goal. The auditorium with its three rows of boxes was small and, of course, temporary. Smetana, who had finally obtained the post of *Kapellmeister* there in 1866, campaigned tirelessly for the building of a representative national theatre and when finally in 1868 its foundation stone was laid, the occasion was celebrated like a national festival

There is a great tradition of composers playing the viola, and it has often been suggested that this has to do with how the instrument is placed within orchestral and instrumental textures. Beethoven began his career as a viola-player in the electoral orchestra in Bonn and Mozart revealed his great love of playing the instrument in his exquisite 'Kegelstatt' Trio. In the 20th century, Schoenberg, Bridge and Britten all played it, whilst Paul Hindemith was the leading composer-violist until the rise of the Australian Brett Dean.

and a procession wound its way right through the inner city.

Dvořák was directly involved in all this, but only in the humble capacity of an orchestral violist. His first compositions, apart from some early dances, are chamber music and symphonies written without any hope of performance, but he was already setting out, instinctively sure-footed, on the path which led to his greatest works. His op 1 was the 1861 String Quintet, the op 2 in A major followed the next year as the first of his 14 string quartets. Although trained as an organist he did not apply his first independent ideas to that instrument, for its objective tones and the polyphonic structure of typical organ music were not as close to his heart as the individual sound and innate melody of string instruments. His lifelong worship of Mozart, Beethoven and Schubert, the great masters of the string quartet, is reflected in this early chamber music. 'Bohu díky' ('Thanks be to God') – the pious words which he often wrote at the end of his scores – first appears on the manuscript of op 2.

Beethoven's lofty example is also stamped on Dvořák's First Symphony. The keys of the four movements – C minor, A-flat major, C minor, C major – are reminiscent of Beethoven's Fifth Symphony and the broad phrases which simply cannot find their resolution recall Schubert's 'celestial longueur'. This blissful style of music is even less restrained in the First Cello Concerto, from the same productive year of 1865. Dvořák's emotion over his unhappy love for Josefina overflows into the intimate lyricism of song. His first song cycle *Cypresses (Cypřiše),* composed in the summer of 1865, sets to music 18 mournfully romantic poems by the lyric poet and novelist Gustav Pfleger-Moravský with unaffected vocal melodies and elementary piano accompaniments. For sentimental reasons he clung to these songs and later developed several of them in different ways – the parsimony of a spendthrift. In this fruitful year he produced a Second Symphony, in B-flat major. It was yet another composition destined to be put into storage and even intended to be burnt (it was rescued by chance). It is already more personal in its blend of the Viennese and the Bohemian. Šourek called it Dvořák's *Pastorale* and compared his First Symphony with Beethoven's Fifth.

The three String Quartets in D major, B-flat major and E minor which followed in 1869 and 1870 announce the deeply stirring experiences of Dvořák's years of turmoil. Here the clear harmony associated with Viennese classicism and Czech folk song is enriched with chromaticism, and a kind of 'endless melody' in this chamber music is a nod towards Wagner and Liszt. It blossomed in Dvořák's hands. His admiration for the 'new Germans' did not prevent him from building the third movement of the D major quartet around the tune of the Slav battle-song *Hej Slované* (even more obviously than Beethoven choosing a Russian theme for his second Razumovsky Quartet). The Slav tune had emotional overtones for Dvořák, as it was the unofficial anthem of revolutionary Poland, *Poland is not yet lost (Jeszce Polska niezgyniela)*, but much more significant was the element of 'new German' style in this quartet.

In 1863 Wagner conducted a concert of his own works in Prague – a great occasion for the city and an experience for Dvořák, who was also playing in the orchestra when Liszt's oratorio *Die heilige Elisabeth (Saint Elizabeth)* was performed under Smetana's baton. In the envied German theatre he encountered the then revolutionary operas of Wagner – *Der fliegende Holländer, Tannhäuser, Lohengrin* and lastly *Die Meistersinger von Nürnberg* – and was fascinated by them. He personally participated in the intellectual struggle over the nature of independent Czech opera between the conservative Old Czechs, represented by the influential politician František Ladislav Rieger, and the Young Czechs, led by Smetana. The Old Czechs conceived it as a medley of folk tunes but Smetana, the Wagnerian, refuted them in practice by unswervingly swearing by the master's principles in his operas, which the Czechs called 'zpěvohry' (operettas). Even the popular *Bartered Bride* with its tuneful numbers was initially rejected as being 'un-Czech' and his *Dalibor*, the first great Czech heroic opera, did not win success for years and led to its composer acquiring the absurd reputation of a 'Germaniser' – a betrayer of the true Czech cause.

The humble violist, Dvořák, frankly worshipped the old master under whose baton he played – even though for a while he resented what he considered insufficient support for his own operas – and they often met at the musicians' table in the Vienna Coffee House on the corner of Wenceslas Square. If he had really been such a simple 'note-smith' as he was said to be, he would have found it easier, when he stepped out of the orchestra pit and onto the creative musical stage, to allow himself to be drawn into the popular Czech trend and write traditional operas, as his friends were doing. For instance, Karel Bendl's *Lejla* and Karel Šebor's patriotic *Drahomíra* were supplementing the sparse Czech repertory at the Provisional Theatre. However, in his first attempts at opera Dvořák remained true to himself and his convictions without in the slightest setting his sights on short-term success. In the Provisional Theatre everything was sung in Czech but for the text of his first opera Dvořák chose the play *Alfred* by Theodor Körner (a poet of the German war of liberation, who had died young) and adapted it himself in German – an example of utter naivety, as there was not the slightest chance of its being performed.[10] The play dealt with a heroic episode from 9th-century English history and the score was dominated by Wagnerian recitatives and early romantic leitmotifs. As a matter of curiosity, the dominant leitmotif (or rather, signature tune) for the hero Alfred the Great anticipated the tune of the Socialist 'Internationale'.

The score of *Alfred* went into storage but Dvořák was not discouraged from trying again a year later (1871) to write another

Wagnerian opera, *King and Charcoal Burner (Král a uhlíř)*, to an amateur libretto by the lawyer Bernard Guldener (as a humble orchestral musician Dvořák was hardly in a position to demand literary excellence!), which told of the legendary meeting of two good men – one great and one

humble. The Wagnerian orchestration is modelled on *Die Meistersinger*, with folk style themes woven in. The manuscript was accepted and rehearsals began but were broken off because the performers found the music too difficult. Smetana, who was conducting, looked on it with favour but maintained – rightly – 'This is a serious piece of work, full of marvellous invention, but I do not think it will be performed.'[11] Dvořák withdrew the piece but stubbornly retained the inadequate

Portrait of Antonín Dvořák

libretto and set it again from start to finish, this time as an unpretentious piece with musical numbers – unique in operatic history. In this form it was first performed at the Provisional Theatre in 1874 but its initial success did not last.

Smetana had already performed the overture in a concert in 1872, shortly after the public had learnt of the existence of Antonín Dvořák, a composer no longer in his first youth. In 1871 the influential musical impresario and critic Dr Ludevít Procházka had written about the composition of *King and Charcoal Burner* in the journal *Hudební listy* and the same year saw the first public performance of an as yet unpublished Dvořák composition – a song for keyboard. He agreed to the publication of his more mature cycle of six songs from the Dvůr Králové manuscript –

that patriotic forgery by Hanka which Dvořák, like all his contemporaries, took to be genuine old Czech poetry – without asking for a fee.

These were years of searching and of passionate fascination with Wagner, during which, in 1872, he had already composed the choral work *Hymnus* which was later to signal his breakthrough to fame and simultaneously his release from Wagner's spell. Neither the unpublished products of his storm and stress years nor the lessons he had learnt from the 'new German' school were in vain. Without his Wagner experience Dvořák's orchestration would certainly not have become so richly colourful and it is no coincidence that in old age, after his symphonies, he should have composed neo-romantic tone poems. Šourek was right when he summed it up: 'If it seemed strange to anyone decades later that the apparently conservative Dvořák should have relied in his last operas and his symphonic poems on the reforming principles which underlie Wagner's and Liszt's works, the explanation that this was no sudden, unprepared and illogical development can be found in his early creative period. In this light even those early compositions can be seen as decidedly significant in the history of his development.'[12]

First Successes 1873–1877

Dvořák was depressed by the rejection of his opera *King and Charcoal Burner* and upset over his unhappy love affair. Although his stored compositions were useful as practice, his complete obscurity and exclusion from musical life hurt even such a modest, unassuming man as he was. But his urge to compose was boundless – he just *had* to write, never mind whether there was any chance of performance – and as for the manuscripts, he did not care much about them. The carefree attitude of Puccini's young bohemians is echoed in something Dvořák said later in his life: *On Sundays, when we wanted to eat dumplings {a Bohemian delicacy}, the maid used to turn confidently to me. I always had paper on me for lighting a fire.*[13] He destroyed many of his early works but fortunately not as many as was originally believed.

In spite of his indifference – whether genuine or defiant – Dvořák must have been enormously elated when one of his compositions at last met with success. At the premiere in 1873 of *Hymnus* in a concert given by the newly founded Hlahol Choir with its splendid complement of 300 voices, this work by a virtually unknown composer was hailed as a triumph. The patriotic circumstances which surrounded it no doubt contributed to its success, for while the Hlahol Choir fulfilled a national function in these first years of Czech resurgence, the poem which Dvořák had set to music – *Heirs of the White Mountain (Dědicové bílé hory)* by Vítězslav Hálek (1835–1874), one of the founders of contemporary Czech poetry – gave the work a strong emotional resonance. It laments the tragic fate of the Czechs after losing the battle of the White Mountain to the Habsburgs and calls for faithfulness to the death and belief in the eternal mother – the Czech people.

'There is only one fatherland, only one mother!' ring out the final words.

Dvořák set these last words to music with enthusiastic exuberance, as indeed he did the whole poem. When out of the gloom of the mourning E-flat minor 'misterioso' the grandiose fortissimo in E-flat major finally surfaces through romantic harmonic modulations and polyphonic flourishes of Handelian clarity, there emerges a naive version of Beethoven's *per aspera ad astra* principle, and this optimism about universal human destiny also serves a narrower nationalism because Dvořák believed unashamedly both in Beethoven and in his own people.

Two weeks later he was to hear the applause again, when his *Notturno for String Orchestra* was performed in a Philharmonic concert. It is a lovely piece whose ravishing parallel sixths in F major he repeated 20 years later in the fourth of his world-famous *Humoresques*. The response must have delighted him and suddenly, overnight, he was famous and fêted. In that year his output was even more abundant than before. The conflict between his fascination with new German music and typical Czech characteristics is demonstrated in his next works. The Piano Quintet in A major, written the previous year in three movements without a scherzo, on the model of Liszt's tone poems, features a sequence of modulations and a finale in 6/8 time which was to become a Dvořák hallmark. In the adagio of the Symphony in E-flat major (which Smetana performed in 1874, thereby dispelling the composer's resentment towards him), the spectre of the Valhalla motif from *Das Rheingold* can be heard in the key and mood of D-flat major. The String Quartet in F minor (which Šourek considered an independent precursor of Smetana's later string quartet *From My Life)* has a joyful finale typical of Dvořák. The A minor String Quartet of 1873 follows the new-German tone poem experiment of fusing four movements into one.

It should be noted that though these may be immature works,

Anna Cermakova, she and Dvořák were married in 1873

they are among the first pieces of Czech music, as are those which immediately followed: the first Czech symphony, string quartet, piano trio and complete choral work. This was a period of firsts for their creator, too, for the early 1870s saw the first public performance of one of his compositions, the publication of a song, *The Lark*, the performance of a major work and the printing of another (the A minor String Quartet). In addition, all these compositions, including the Piano Concerto in G minor and the first Rhapsody, surpassed rather than followed the older Smetana, who had been called the creator of Czech national music.

These early successes strengthened Dvořák's self-confidence, both artistically and personally. He now felt he was in a position to set up housekeeping – no light decision, in view of his deeply religious views on marriage – and on 17 November 1873 he married Anna Čermáková. The young couple first went to live with her parents but a few months later moved into their own apartment, 14 Na Rybníčku in the Nové Město, and three years later to no 10 Korntorgasse (now Žitná) – both modest dwellings in blocks of rented flats.

This happy and lasting marriage was overshadowed by the early deaths of the first three children. In the year after he married Dvořák took a post as organist at the parish church of St Adalbert

Dvořák's home in Nove Mesto, Prague

where he remained until 1877. He was not an outstanding organist; Janáček, who was studying in Prague at the time, criticised his improvisations as 'restrained' and academic, but still the two of them went on a walking tour together in 1877 through Central and Southern Bohemia.

The main source of the family's income came from his giving piano lessons and later playing the viola in the private concerts arranged by the German-Bohemian Prague industrialist Josef Portheim. From 1875 this was supplemented by an annual grant of 400 guilders from the Vienna Ministry of Culture, which had set this sum aside since 1863 for promising Czech artists, though not necessarily for musicians. It was renewed several times and was the most lavish payment he had ever received. He had submitted his E-flat Symphony to the Grants Commission, where the decision rested

Leoš Janáček (1854–1928) stands out as the most important figure in Czech music after Dvořák. His early works, particularly the Suite and Serenade for String Orchestra, are very much in the lyrical language of his German and Czech contemporaries. But his late instrumental works, such as the two quartets and the wind sextet *Mládí* (Youth) are regarded as startlingly innovative to this day. His vocal and instrumental music became uniquely influenced by the speech rhythms of his native Moravia, and the two late string quartets represent the most passionate outpouring from an older composer since César Franck. Writing about Dvořák he said: ' Do you know what it is like when someone takes the words out of your mouth before

you speak them? This is how I always felt in Dvořák's company . . . he has taken his melodies from my heart.'

with the Vienna Director of the Court Opera, Johann Ritter von Herbeck, Johannes Brahms (a vitally decisive moment for Dvořák's future career) and Eduard Hanslick, a native of Prague and the doyen of music critics, who was later unjustly denounced as being anti-Wagner. Hanslick must have had an uncanny feel for quality, as he detected something exceptional in the manuscript of a completely unknown composer. He wrote: 'Among the applications for this grant, which each year flow into the Ministry weighed down with scores, most usually come from composers who only possess the first two of the official prerequisites: youth, lack of means and talent, but not the third. So it was a pleasant surprise for us when one day a Prague candidate, Anton Dvořák, sent in evidence of a considerable talent for composition, even though it as yet lacked maturity.'[14]

Dvořák's output became more prolific than ever, now that his livelihood was secure and his name known, at least in Prague. In the mid-1870s, his passion for Wagner having abated, he returned to Beethoven, Schubert and Schumann as his models – thereby, rather than regressing, seeking and finding his own identity. Undoubtedly Smetana's example as an opera composer contributed to this; having listened attentively to repeated performances of *The Bartered Bride* Dvořák, like most Czechs, realised that the accusations of Wagnerianism were ridiculous and when the more Mozartian comic opera *The Two Widows (Dvě vdovy)* came out in 1874 he was totally convinced that truly Czech music was not to be achieved through imitating Wagner's music-dramas nor through producing potpourris of Czech folk songs, but only by giving birth to new creations. Around the end of 1873 Šourek recognised the crisis Dvořák was going through: 'Once again the spirit of Beethoven's and Schubert's music hovers over his [Dvořák's] compositions, not taking complete possession of them as at first but, together with the spirit of Smetana, shedding an indefinable illumination over his work . . . A tranquillity is beginning to pervade Dvořák's music, for he now acknowledges his own ability and is the master of his material, thereby giving it clarity and weight, while his means of expression govern the rules for their economical and practical use.'[15]

This description fits a number of compositions from this period: his Fourth Symphony in D minor, composed in 1874, the andante of which is his first variation movement he wrote; the first Rhapsody in A minor which, according to a notice in the journal *Dalibor*, was to be the first of a cycle of Slav rhapsodies 'somewhat in the manner of Liszt's rhapsodies on Hungarian folk songs'; the four-movement String Quartet in A minor, his second in that key, written with his customary energy in ten days; and even more the chamber music he wrote in 1875 – the classical, light-hearted String Quintet in G major, the Piano Trio in B-flat major, followed a year later by another in G minor, (the presto scherzo sounds like a forerunner of the famous Slavonic Dances), the rarely played Piano Quartet in D major and the String Quartet in E major. The String Serenade, a five-movement suite which was to become one of his most popular pieces, also has an entirely classical calm about it and represents an ideal example of superb, inspired light music. The F major Symphony, composed in the summer of 1875, has been compared with Beethoven's Pastoral Symphony because of its key but it is in fact a transitional piece, though approaching the quality of the composer's major works. Its andante is a typical Dvořák 'dumka', contrasting an elegiac element with a high-spirited dance.

Dvořák plunged into writing operas with new courage. His depressing experiences to date must have frightened him off and he still could not find a serviceable libretto, as soon became apparent. To a Czech composer, however, the highest goal must have seemed to be to show one's ability to compose operas; the 'temple' of the National Theatre was already being built and Smetana's growing reputation spurred him on. That Dvořák first contented himself with a comic one-act folk opera shows that he had an eye for practical considerations as well as marking the new course he was steering away from Wagner. *The Stubborn Lovers (Tvrdé palice)*, to a fairly satisfactory libretto he commissioned from Josef Štolba, a notary and author of farces, is set in the working-class milieu Dvořák knew well: two young lovers, who at first do not want to have anything to do with each other, are made jealous by a cunning uncle who steers them into each other's arms – arms which only their stubbornness had kept closed. The 16 short scenes are not distinguished by any spark of genius, but by their supple arioso style and by the composer refusing to use secco recitative to link his numbers (a method which even Smetana had found essential at that time). Dvořák had to wait seven years for its first performance and then in 1881 it swiftly vanished from the stage.

Meanwhile Dvořák had ventured on a heroic subject in his *Vanda* (premiere 1876), but it was a very bad choice. The journalist Václav Beneš Šumavský had cobbled together a linguistically turgid and dramatically amateurish libretto based on a story from prehistory which told of the Polish Princess Vanda who loved her compatriot Sir Slavoj, but was being pressed into marriage by Sir Roderich, a German. The foreign invaders were defeated but Vanda had dedicated herself to the gods and threw herself into the Vistula. The contemporaneous Czech enthusiasm for the Poles as victims of Russian repression may explain his choice of material but it is still not clear how he could waste so much energy on the score (five whole acts), which is an impersonal mishmash of Smetana, Wagner and Meyerbeer.

Dvořák showed an almost equal lack of critical sense when, shortly afterwards, he set to music a libretto called *The Cunning Peasant (Šelma sedlák)* by a not untalented but megalomaniac 23-year old writer and medical student called Josef Otakar Vesely. This young man, who was to die of tuberculosis three years later, felt he was born to be the 'Saviour of our wretched literature'. However as Dvořák's partner, he produced a text of startling naivety whose plot is a mixture of *The Marriage of Figaro* (with a philandering Count) and *The Bartered Bride* (from which he even copied the names of the two rivals, Jeník and Václav). Dvořák was not worried by either the banal language or the gauche dramatic development. He felt at home in this healthy, rustic world of harmless pranks and lavished on it by far the best music he had so far written for the stage. It is full of wit and feeling and superbly crafted. Choruses and ensembles, tuneful arias, a tender E-flat major duet for the lovers, flowing melodies and stirring rhythms – all hopelessly tied to a worthless libretto. The friendly applause at the 1878 premiere could not rescue the unrescuable in the long run, but nevertheless this was Dvořák's first opera to appear on the stage abroad. In 1882 Ernst von Schuch performed it in Dresden in a version desolately transplanted from Bohemia to Upper Austria; a year later it appeared in Hamburg and three years afterwards at the Vienna State Opera, where it was unsympathetically directed and was not a success. Hanslick poured his scorn over the bungled German text and said that this piece of Bohemian country life should not be uprooted out of its native soil.[16] Agreeing with the Czech experts on Dvořák that this impossible libretto dragged down the sparkling music, the author of this book, Oskar Honolka, freely adapted the libretto to fit the score and under the title *Der Schelm und die Bauern (The Rascal and the Peasants)* Dvořák's first operatic masterpiece was eventually to flourish in Germany.[17]

Dvořák was luckier with his works for the concert stage in the 1870s, though less with his only Piano Concerto in G minor (1876) than with two important vocal works. The Piano Concerto is remarkable for a certain similarity to Brahms; like him, Dvořák wrote a sort of symphony with piano obbligato and the solo part is unrewarding, which is why it is mostly played in the arrangement by Vilém Kurz, a piano professor. At the time Dvořák was giving piano lessons in the house of a wealthy merchant, Jan Neff, who with his wife and their governess liked singing duets and had soon exhausted the existing repertoire.

The Czech-born critic Eduard Hanslick (1825–1904), studied law and philosophy in Vienna and Prague, also studying the piano under Tomášek. He did more than any other writer to further the dispute as to the nature of true German music in the second half of the 19th century. A virulent opponent of the Liszt–Wagner movement, he was one of the earliest supporters of Schumann, and lectured at Prague, Vienna and Cologne between 1859–63. His review of Adolf Brodsky's premiere of the Tchaikovsky violin concerto is legendary: 'The violin is no longer played . . . it is yanked about . . . beaten black and blue.'

They turned to their composer–teacher and asked him to arrange a few folk songs for two voices. Marie Neff remembers: 'Our governess had borrowed Sušil's collection, chose 15 songs she liked and Dvořák promised to write a second voice part and an accompaniment to them After a few days, however, he had thought the matter over. *I am not going to do it,* he explained. *If you like, I will write you some songs in my own style but I will not add a second voice part to these.*[18]

This decision of Dvořák's is not just evidence of his artistic integrity; composing Czech national music was not as easy as the patriotic 'old Czechs' made out. Smetana declined to elaborate on folk tunes in his operas and only in his comic opera *The Kiss (Hubička)* did he include an old lullaby, following it immediately with another of his own invention, as though he wanted to say: look, I may be called a Wagnerian but I can do this just as well! Dvořák did the same with the folk song collection of the Moravian priest František Sušil; he set the old words afresh with an inspired insight into the idiosyncrasies of Moravian folk music, which differed in many ways from the Bohemian – for instance, in a preference for greater intervals, and different stresses.

Using as a basis the three Duets op 20, written in the spring of 1875, he developed over the next three years the cycle which established his international fame – *Moravian Duets (Moravské dvojzěv).*[19] The songs are predominantly sunny in mood but not without shadows – in fact, absolutely genuine: love as delight, longing and lament, teasing, a soldier's destiny and nature, all in a tender, symbolic blend. Dvořák conveyed the direct impact of this lyricism in tunes which sound like folk songs. The piano part is easy and the imitative vocal line, though often elaborated, almost always matches the words of the poems. This is a stroke of genius in an exceptional period when art and folklore were ideally blending. The next generation (that of Gustav Mahler) could only convey through the distorting mirror of intellect their longing for simplicity and popular culture – that nostalgia which feeds on childhood impressions of the sentimental sounds of horn and trumpets.

The second vocal composition which made Dvořák famous, the *Stabat Mater*, is a magnificent work, owing a certain detachment to its Latin text but imbued with a deep spirituality by the composer's personal involvement. In 1876, in the aftermath of the death of his baby daughter Josefa, he sketched out his setting of the medieval text by Jacopone da Todi, which had been set by many early composers, including Pergolesi and Rossini. A year and a half later the young family suffered two more terrible blows: the eleven-month old Růžena died after drinking a solution of phosphorus when no-one was watching her and three weeks later chickenpox carried off their first child, Otakar, at the age of three and a half. Dvořák the Catholic sought refuge in his religion. He took out his sketches and the whole burden of his grief and faith dissolved into the monastic phrases on the suffering of 'Our Lady Mother of Sorrows'.

The *Stabat Mater* is not just the first great sacred work in Czech music; the powerful dimensions of its ten sections for chorus, soloists and orchestra (it lasts 90 minutes) make it also the first climax in Dvořák's vocal work. Although in the interests of objectivity the composer renounced any references to folk music, he was still true to his own style which had by now become contrapuntally more secure. Even in the realm of sacred music orientated towards Bach, Handel and Beethoven's *Missa Solemnis*, Dvořák displays above all his unmistakable personality as a melodist.

The Symphonic Variations, 28 variants on a Czech folk song dating from the end of 1877, show Dvořák at the peak of his instrumental mastery. His twelve *Evening Songs (Večerni pisně)* after Vitězslav Hálek, various smaller compositions for chorus and piano and above all his String Quartet in D minor (his ninth and possibly his first truly mature quartet, with cantabile first movement, a profound adagio and a Slavonic dance in the allegretto scherzando), together with some relatively minor works, bear witness to the composer's boundless wealth of creativity.

Despite this Dvořák was still relatively unknown internationally, only esteemed as a musician by his compatriots, but soon the world was to recognise that in provincial obscurity a master was growing to maturity.

Brahms and the 'Slavonic Period' 1877–1884

. . . But an even greater good fortune is the favour which you, highly respected Sir, have shown towards my humble talent and also the approval which my Bohemian duet songs have found in your eminence's sight (according to a letter from Professor Hanslick). The Professor has now advised me to make a German translation of these songs and informs me that you, honoured Sir, might be good enough to recommend them to your publishers. This is my only other request to you, to help me in this way as well, as it is of great importance to me. It would truly be of inestimable value, not just for me but for my beloved fatherland, if you, esteemed maestro, whose works give such immense joy to the whole musical world, were to introduce me into it.

While beseeching your honour for your highly valued favour, in the future as well, I beg you at the same time for your kind permission to lay before you some of my chamber-music and instrumental compositions for your gracious consideration.

I have the honour to remain, with the deepest respect, your most humble servant
Anton Dvořák.[20]

With this reverential letter to Brahms there began at the end of 1877 a correspondence between two great composers and a lifelong professional friendship characterised by generous mutual respect. Dvořák's letter was occasioned by Brahms's deciding vote in awarding him the grant from the Viennese Education Ministry. Dvořák started gratefully and always remained so – understandably, for not only did he owe to Brahms's advocacy the grant which made him partially independent to lead a very modest life, but also the leap he now made over the narrow boundaries of his homeland, out of the provinces and into the wider musical world. That international recognition which Smetana never attained in his lifetime came to Dvořák through Brahms's beneficent intervention.

This letter asking for patronage was not in vain. More or less simultaneously with his polite reply to Dvořák Brahms wrote to Fritz Simrock (1838–1901), the leading Leipzig publisher: '. . . Dvořák has written all sorts of music, operas (Bohemian), symphonies, quartets and piano pieces. In any case he is a very talented man – and poor with it! Please bear that in mind! . . .'[21]

Until then Dvořák's name as a composer had only been known in the provincial city of Prague, but now he suddenly became one of the names on the list of the internationally influential publishing house of Simrock. He travelled to Vienna to thank Brahms, but found he was away from home. Later Brahms visited Dvořák in Prague and the latter returned the visit in Vienna. They met seldom but their lifelong friendship never faltered. Brahms, who was eight years older, was always a kind of father figure to Dvořák, who accepted his generosity with heartfelt gratitude.

They made a strange pair of friends. One a North German, influenced in his youth by the highly cultivated circle around Robert and Clara Schumann, well versed in literature and philosophy, contemplating and brooding over music, deeply sceptical, non-religious; the other a Czech from artisan stock, raised in a

In 1897, Brahms persuaded the cellist of the Joachim Quartet, Robert Hausmann, to come to his rooms and play through the Czech Antonín Dvořák's Cello Concerto with him at the piano. Afterwards, he exclaimed: 'Had I known that such a 'cello concerto as that could have been written, I could have tried to compose one myself.' Dvořák dedicated his D minor Quartet op 34 to Brahms in 1877, in gratitude for the support that Brahms had given him, and which he continued to give for the rest of his life, consistently promoting the performance and publication of his music.

narrow cultural milieu, whose literary taste was never properly developed, whose inner potential could only find its outlet in music (in Janáček's opinion 'his intelligence was . . . of a very particular kind . . . he thought exclusively in notation, nothing else existed for him'[22], a Catholic of totally sincere piety who even in old age said of his friend with complete incomprehension: *Such a man, such a soul – and he believes in nothing, he believes in nothing!*[23]

What had the two men to offer each other? Above all, human affection. Brahms's readiness to help went so far as to invite Dvořák to move to Vienna with his whole family at his expense ('My fortune is at your disposal') and when Dvořák was in America, he corrected urgently needed proofs for him. Artistically Brahms could acknowledge the younger man as a colleague, in that both were swimming against the 'new-German' tide of the time through their chamber music and symphonies, and realising in the most precise manner the 'musically thrilling forms' of absolute music which was the aesthetic principle of Brahms's friend Hanslick. Dvořák's veneration for Wagner did not seem to trouble Brahms, whose delight in the freshness of the Czech composer's plethora of musical ideas was as genuine and lasting as the latter's admiration of his patron's mastery.

Though the younger man did learn from the older, unmistakably Brahmsian features cannot be found in his works; the greater artistic technique in melody and development in Dvořák's mature compositions is not only modelled on Brahms. It was as impossible for Dvořák to imitate

'Absolute music' is usually used to define music that is free of any programmatic associations, pictorial evocations or poetic ideas. The relative merits of the two aesthetics of programmatic and absolute music defined the battle lines that separated the followers of Wagner and Liszt on the one hand, and those of Schumann and Brahms on the other. This debate raged well into the 20th century, and to a degree has been reanimated since the rise of cinema, which co-opts instrumental music for illustrative purposes.

the spirituality in Brahms's keyboard and symphonic invention as it was for the German to reproduce the naivety of the Czech's melodic themes and close affinity with folklore. Criticism was offered in mutual friendship and accepted with gratitude. This is how Brahms reacted when Dvořák dedicated his String Quartet in D minor to him: 'You write somewhat hastily, but when later on you put in the sharps, flats and naturals you may sometimes see the notes themselves and the lines of the individual parts, etc with greater insight. Please excuse me; it is very presumptuous of me to make such comments about these things to a man like you!'[24] But the object of his rebuke actually thanked him a year later! *Most revered master! When you were last in Prague you were kind enough to bring to my attention several points in my works and I can only thank you sincerely, for I have now seen many bad notes and replaced them . . .*[25]

Simrock now came to Prague in person to finalise the contracts with Dvořák. Initially he made it clear to the composer that in Germany he was an unknown beginner and paid him no fee for either the *Moravian Duets* or the first piano series of Slavonic Dances. Later he paid him well – 1000 marks (500 guilders) for the Violin Concerto and 6000 marks for the D minor Symphony. Their collaboration was extremely beneficial to both partners: the composer came out into the world and the publisher gained a new and successful name. Out of their business dealings grew a genuine friendship and Dvořák often addressed Simrock in his letters with the affectionate Czech nickname of 'dear Fricku'. Dvořák's circumstances soon improved dramatically and a friend related how in 1878 he triumphantly showed the friends gather in their regular café his first fee from Simrock (in fact his first fee ever worth mentioning) – 300 marks for the orchestral version of the Slavonic Dances. As a sign of his gradually growing income, he moved two years later from the back courtyard in the Korntorgasse (Žitná) into a larger apartment on the second floor of the same house, where he had a roomy study with desk and grand piano and where he was to live for the rest of his life when in Prague. In the summer of 1878 came another daughter, Otilie, who was to marry the composer Josef Suk. Dvořák was now a happy family man, basking in domestic contentment and professional success, enjoying early morning birdsong in the leafy Karlova Naměsti a few steps from the house and indulging his hobby for hours on end at the nearby Franz-Joseph Station (now the main railway station of Prague). He had a passion for locomotives and would note down the most complicated serial numbers and even the names of the drivers.

Josef Suk (1874–1935) studied composition with Dvořák from 1891–2, and began his career playing second violin in his violin teacher Wihan's acclaimed quartet, which was renamed the Bohemian Quartet in 1892. He married Otilie, Dvořák's daughter in 1898. He served both as Professor of Composition and Rector at the Prague Conservatoire. His Serenade for String Orchestra is regarded as almost equal to Dvořák's and in recent years, his symphonic works have achieved great acclaim in the West, especially *Asrael*, his second symphony.

Simrock had now brought out the *Moravian Duets* recommended by Brahms and they sold so well that he commissioned Dvořák to write some dances in the style of Brahms's Hungarian Dances, also for piano duet but in Slavonic, or Bohemian, style. The resultant Slavonic Dances have become Dvořák's most popular work. Following on the tremendous success of the piano version, he orchestrated the first series of eight in 1878 and in 1886 added eight more, thereby creating 16 masterpieces of melodic, rhythmic and tonal invention, surpassing Brahms's Hungarian Dances, because the latter simply dressed up existing folk tunes in superb music, while Dvořák invented the tunes himself.

Popular dances from Bohemia and other Slavonic cultures were his models, but the fact that Dvořák elaborated on them without sacrificing any of their 'divine naturalness'[26] speaks for his artistry and instinctive affinity with genuine folklore. Unlike Brahms, who loved folk songs, he did not need to track down these airs from a past golden age, because he carried in his heart and ears the tunes which were still being sung and danced in the countryside. The second, more richly elaborated, series features kolos, polonaises, odzemeks, etc from other Slav countries, while the first, like Smetana's piano suite, could be described as Czech, for it is made up of Bohemian and Moravian dances such as the polka, the skočna and the gentle, minuet-style sousedská and begins and ends with a furiant, an incisively rhythmic dance, whose main characteristic is a sequence of alternating bars in 3/2 and 3/4 time, marked by accents.

In the years which followed Dvořák incorporated variations on all these dances into his chamber and symphonic music and this time of overflowing joy in creativity and masterpieces can rightly be called his Slavonic period. No longer did he need to put his compositions into storage; everything he composed was performed at once in Germany and in Vienna, so that he could hardly keep up with the commissions. The increasing enthusiasm for his orchestral works shown by prominent German conductors like Hans Richter, Hans von Bülow and Arthur Nikisch helped to shape his course towards fame throughout Europe.

Almost simultaneously with the Slavonic Dances he was writing other essentially Czech works, the first being the String Serenade in D minor for wind with cello and double bass – a cheerful piece, in spite of its key, which seems to reflect Mozart's radiance (in fact, the inspiration for it came from a Mozart concert he attended in Vienna). Thereafter came the three Slavonic Rhapsodies which, though the composer did not comment any further on their content, were nevertheless a series of ballad-like symphonic tone poems in the manner of Smetana's *Má Vlast*. The emotional formality of the first in D major is reminiscent of

Joseph Joachim (1831–1907) was perhaps the greatest master of the violin of any generation. He came to international acclaim, aged twelve, with a performance of the then neglected Beethoven Violin Concerto at the Philharmonic Society in London, conducted by Mendelssohn. His impact on serious music-making cannot be underestimated, ranging from his resuscitation of the violin works of Bach, to his work with living composers, including Liszt, Wagner, Brahms, Schumann, Dvořák and Clara Schumann. His quartet playing set a standard of performance and musical ethics which has never been superseded, and was largely responsible for establishing Dvořák's quartets in the Western European concert repertoire.

Joseph Joachim cartooned by Spy in *Vanity Fair* 1905

Vyšehrad, the sombrely accentuated G minor rhapsody evokes a mythical tragedy and that in A-flat major chivalrous pageantry. Liszt's Rhapsodies provided him with models but the straightforward ternary and rondo structures and the melodies are entirely his own. Smetana felt – quite groundlessly – that in starting the third rhapsody with a harp solo Dvořák was plagiarising his *Vyšehrad*. The old maestro, by then completely deaf and living alone in the country, was embittered by his sufferings and quite jealous of Dvořák's sudden rise to fame, but nevertheless he showed his joy in his compatriot's international success and was unstinting in his praise for the Slavonic Dances, when at his request he was sent the score ('the young gentlemen composers should at least show old Smetana their work').

The String Sextet in A major – Dvořák's key for happiness and inner harmony – has a dumka (so marked for the first time) as its second movement and a furiant for its presto. It is significant, not only as his first chamber work to be played abroad, but also because the famous violinist Joseph Joachim (1831–1907) and his quartet performed it in Berlin. Joachim, who had had a hand in writing the solo part of Brahms's Violin Concerto, also acted as Dvořák's mentor on his Violin Concerto in A minor and on his advice the composer revised not only the solo part but the entire work. It can hardly have been through Brahms's direct influence that the solo violin is integrated into the orchestra, because Dvořák had already done this in his Piano Concerto and the thematic material, including a rushing furiant in the finale, is once again unmistakably Dvořák's own. Thanks to this collaboration with the experienced virtuoso the solo part is very effective; however, it was not Joachim but the young Czech violinist František Ondříček who first performed it in 1883 and launched it on its glorious career.

Work followed work: the lovely Bagatelles for two violins, cello and harmonium, the three Modern Greek Songs (Tři novořecké básně) for baritone and piano and later the Gypsy Songs (Cigánské melodie) – Dvořák's best vocal compositions to date – which tell of the gypsies' love for music in strophic verse and, curiously enough, were composed to a German translation of the verses made by the Czech poet Adolf Heyduk. The Choral Society Hlahol commissioned him to write a setting of the 149th Psalm, the old, traditional sequences of which are a belated homage to Handel. The Czech Suite in D major for chamber orchestra is a lovely serenade with one of the most fiery of Dvořák's furiants as the presto finale. Smaller piano pieces were overshadowed by a new String Quartet in E-flat major, commissioned by the

Florentine String Quartet, a sunny, good-humoured composition.

The D major Symphony of 1880 could be described in the same terms and the Czechs count it among his four last, great symphonies. The main theme of the first movement recalls the finale of Schumann's *Papillons* but is spun out in Dvořák's own style and a presto-furiant takes the place of the scherzo. 'In this symphony dwell the gaiety, humour and passion of the Czech people', enthused Šourek.[27] Hans Richter was no less enthusiastic when he performed it in London. *Richter liked the symphony enormously and embraced me after each movement*, wrote Dvořák after playing the new work through to the conductor when visiting him in Vienna. Out of the euphoria engendered by his stream of successes that year grew another String Quartet in C major from whose inspiration and mature, polished structure one would never guess that it had been written in a few days, and each of the first two movements in just two days! With less commitment the composer dutifully accepted the theatre director's commission to write incidental music for the play *Josef Kajetán Tyl* by Frans Ferdinand Šamberk – a sentimental dramatisation of the life of Tyl, an early 19th century pioneer of the Czech theatre. Tyl wrote the words of the song *Where is my homeland (Kde domov můj),* which later became the Czech national anthem, and Dvořák's working of František Škroup's popular air, combined with the folk tune *In our Courtyard*, survives as an overture though the play has long vanished. Simrock published it under the incorrect German title *Mein Heim,* meaning 'my home' which, translated back for Czech performances as *Má Vlast,* was taken as an unethical abuse of the name of Smetana's symphonic cycle and aroused smouldering petty jealousies between the supporters of Smetana and Dvořák, though the latter was in no way to blame.

Dvořák relaxed after his frequent professional travels to Berlin, Dresden, Vienna, Wiesbaden and Cologne by making smaller trips in the countryside near his home. With his friend Alois

Göbl, a teacher and later an estate manager, he went to the Bohemian Woods and there noted down his impressions of nature in piano pieces for four hands. He liked staying at Meierhof, near Sychrov in Northern Bohemia, where his friend was manager, and even more on his brother-in-law Count Kaunitz's property in Vysoká, near the Southern Bohemian mining town of Příbram, but there were other, less enjoyable journeys to make from Prague, where he had chosen to live. In 1880 he travelled to Zlonice to play the piano at a benefit concert in honour of his old teacher Liehmann, who had died at a great age, and two years later to the little coal town of Kladno where his beloved mother died at the age of 64. His father, whom Dvořák was supporting financially, was eking out a livelihood with difficulty by playing the zither, having had to give up his job as an innkeeper, and the son sublimated these depressing experiences spontaneously and simply in music. The Piano Trio in F minor, written at the beginning of 1883, is a spacious, substantial work which reflects the composer's state of mind in passionate dissonances, but soon afterwards he could not resist writing a Scherzo Capriccioso which sparkles with life throughout.

In between lies a new opera, *Dimitrij*, which was to represent both his most glowing success in Prague and also a bitter disappointment. His hopes of it achieving a breakthrough in Germany similar to that of his concert works remained unfulfilled. The splendid dedication of the National Theatre on the Vltava Embankment with Smetana's festival opera *Libuše* in 1881 gave Dvořák's dramatic ambitions fresh impetus. He had for a while played with the idea of composing music to German libretti for performance in Germany but now his own Czech stage beckoned.

It was a national catastrophe when the theatre burned down two months after its opening but this only stimulated Dvořák's ambition. From all levels of society contributions towards the rebuilding flowed in and two years later it was dedicated for the second time. 'Národ sobě' ('[a gift] to the nation from itself'), declares the proud inscription which can still be read over the classical gable of the proscenium. Only those who appreciate how long the Czechs had been overshadowed by German culture and how belatedly they had acquired their own representative theatre can understand the unique, in the truest sense of the word national, significance of this building – a shrine which went so far as to defy artistic criticism.

Of course Dvořák, being new to fame, was drawn to worship in this temple. *Dimitrij* was intended for the

Marie Červinková-Riegrová, the librettist of Dvořák's opera *The Jacobin*

new theatre but because of the fire the world premiere in October 1882 had to be held in the temporary New Czech Theatre in the Žitná (a copy of the Bayreuth Festspielhaus), where the composer's most ambitious and weightiest stage work was a sensational success and ranked as the second most important Czech tragic opera after Smetana's *Dalibor*. As with the hapless *Vanda,* it was based on a Slav story, but the subject was chosen at random and not because Dvořák was attracted to Russia, as Janáček was. In fact this was the only Russian subject he ever used.

Dvořák's insecurity and lack of critical judgement over the choice of libretti contrast starkly with the decisiveness of born opera composers such as Verdi, Wagner or Puccini. He hesitated for a long time over a text written for him by Julius Zeyer on the Czech myth of *Šarka*, which Janáček later set to music, but his instinct led him to recognise the musical and dramatic potential in the *Dimitrij* of Marie Červinková-Riegrová (1854–1895). The 28-year-old daughter of František Ladislav Rieger, a prominent politician and leader of the 'old Czechs', and wife of the author and landowner Václav Červinka, was herself a writer involved in cultural politics. Her *Dimitrij* libretto was at least superior to the average Czech opera libretto of the day because its structure was dramatically effective and its characters clearly delineated, but this did not make it a masterpiece. It was based on a Czech play by F B Mikovec which was in turn only an adaptation and completion of Schiller's *Demetrius* fragment.

The opera begins where Mussorgsky's *Boris Godunov* breaks off. The usurper Dimitri Voyvoda enters the Kremlin at the side of Marina. Is he really the Tsar's son or is he the lying, false Dimitri? He himself believes in his mission but the conflict between his love for Boris's daughter Xenia and his reliance on Marina's Polish party is his downfall. When Marina takes offence and throws in his face the truth that he is only little Grisha and nothing but the tool of her political ambitions, he collapses and is shot dead by Shuisky.

In this score we see a new side to Dvořák as the self-assured composer of a grand opera with double choruses, sweeping finales and bel canto arias and ensembles. *Dimitrij* cannot be compared with Mussorgsky's *Boris*, which opened up a new world of musical drama with a blend of dilettantism and genius. Here we have a competent musician making use of contemporary achievements from *Lohengrin* to *Aida,* though without compromising his own integrity. The lyricism of Dimitri's D-flat major aria to the holy Kremlin, the emotionally charged warmth of Xenia's music and Marina's triumphant mazurka tempo (a good old friend from the first Slavonic Dance turns up here as a polonaise!) are all so essentially Dvořák that the earlier reproaches of imitating Meyerbeer seem perverse today and can only be explained by the current petty jealousies between Smetana and Dvořák partisans. The leader of the Smetana camp, Zdeněk Nejedlý, went so far as to maintain that *Dimitrij* had been 'directly aimed against Smetana', which was of course far from being Dvořák's intention.

Eduard Hanslick was at the premiere and wrote a very appreciative review in the *Neue Freie Presse*, though with some dramaturgical criticisms, and Dvořák immediately revised the score to take them into account. In 1883 the opera entered the repertoire of the rebuilt National Theatre – the first opera by Dvořák to hold its place there. Hans von Bülow recommended it enthusiastically to Hamburg but no German theatre could decide whether to perform it. When the National Theatre took it to Vienna in 1892 it was clearly overshadowed by *The Bartered Bride*, which had been hailed as a sensational discovery. Dvořák lost confidence and rewrote the score quite radically when he was living in New York, reducing the 'numbers' into a more Wagnerian recitative style (as he understood it) but in so doing he robbed it of its best quality: spontaneous Czech bel canto. This revision was ultimately abandoned.

Dimitrij was Dvořák's dramatic problem child and he clung to it with intense love. *The opera* Dimitrij *is really a work I love and it therefore grieves me all the more that it has so far not been appreciated. According to to Hanslick, as you once reported to me, it was apparently not theatrical and dramatic enough, which annoyed me very much . . .*[28] [It would have given the composer such joy to have seen its eventual triumph outside Bohemia in his lifetime. Surprisingly, this only happened in 1958, when the Norddeutscher Rundfunk produced it in a translation made by the author of this book with such brilliant success that it was soon taken up by networks worldwide.[29] In the following year the Hamburg State Opera staged it in the same translation – the first time it had been seen in a foreign theatre – and public and press alike declared that a jewel of the 'unknown Dvořák' had come to light.[30]]

The conductor and pianist Hans von Bülow (1830–1894) was perhaps the most influential German musician of the 19th century. He studied with Liszt, before making his first concert tour in 1853. Later he married Liszt's daughter Cosima who left him for Wagner after Bülow conducted the premiere of *Die Meistersinger* in 1868. He was the dedicatee of Tchaikovsky's 1st Piano Concerto. Czech-born critic Hanslick wrote: 'His restless, brilliant mind and his reckless energy blow like a north wind, brisk and refreshing, through the stagnant complacency of our everyday musical life.'

But once the National Theatre was finally operational and even before *Dimitrij* appeared in the autumn of 1883, another work by Dvořák – *The Hussite Overture (Husitská)* – had been performed at the Academy in a concert to dedicate the rebuilding of the theatre after the fire. Even Dvořák's friends thought it an aberration that a pious Catholic should glorify the Hussite era, but Hans von Bülow firmly brushed that aside and championed the piece with vigour. Czech supporters of Smetana could not accept that Dvořák could combine the Hussite Chorus *Those who are God's warriors (Ktož jsú boží bjovníce)*, which had provided the musical material for the apotheosis in Smetana's tone poems *Tábor* and *Blaník*, with the older St Wenceslas Chorale. Dvořák was not just exploiting a striking contrast, he had simply followed his instincts and unwittingly fallen between both stools.

This epoch was packed with nationalistic dynamite, for the Bohemian Czechs and Germans were growing apart. In 1882 the Czechs abandoned the ancient University of Charles IV, the first to be built on the soil of the Holy Roman Empire of German Nations, in order to found their own. Germans living in Prague decided to support the foundation of a new modern theatre, which was promptly rejected by the Bohemian 'Landtag' (regional parliament) where Czechs were in the majority. The New German

Theatre (renamed the Smetana Theatre after the Germans were driven out) opened in 1888 as a monument to the private initiative of the German citizens, including the Jews. Though Dvořák was not at all chauvinistic, he became embroiled in this serious nationalistic quarrel. He insisted that in other countries his name should be written correctly in Czech, although he himself did not write the language with any confidence,[31] and he considered his Catholicism no obstacle to showing enthusiasm for the Hussite cause when he received a commission to write the music for a projected drama on the subject. To the Czechs the Hussite period represented a glorious epoch in their national history rather than a movement for religious reform. On the other hand, as a musician and a Catholic Dvořák saw no problem in enlivening the chorus of the Hussite rebels (which was almost automatically associated with anti-German feeling) with the pious chorale of St Wenceslas, an historical symbol of Czechs and Germans living together in harmony, but the Czech nationalists took this amiss. To Dvořák St Wenceslas and Hus were not opposites. When he was looking for a subject for an oratorio, he suggested *St Wenceslas, Hus or someone like that*[32] to the librettist of *Dimitrij.* Two years later he had a 'national political disagreement' with Simrock, who had offended him by refusing sarcastically to print the titles of his compositions in Czech as well as German, but in the end he wrote him a conciliatory letter: *But what do we two care about politics; let's be happy that we can dedicate our services to the beautiful art alone! And let us hope that nations which have and represent art will never perish, however small they are. Please forgive me for this, but I only wanted to tell you that an artist has a fatherland, too, for which he must keep firm faith and a warm heart.*[33]

His Czech patriotism did not in the least affect his friendship with Brahms. In the autumn of 1883 he visited him in Vienna and reported to Simrock: *Every day we met at midday and in the evening and talked about people. He seems to have enjoyed our time together and I am so utterly delighted by his kindness as an artist and a human being that I just love him! What a spirit and soul this man has! You know how reserved he is about his work, even with his best friends and with musicians, but he wasn't like that with me.*[34]

Triumph in England 1884–1889

In the second half of the 19th century it was accepted as normal for a Czech artist, whether composer, writer, painter or singer, to make his or her way onto the international scene via Vienna or one of the German cultural capitals such as Berlin, Dresden or Hamburg, and so it was with Dvořák. The friendly support he had received from Brahms, Joachim, Richter and other influential personalities in German musical life did indeed mean that, unlike Smetana, his name was not only well known at home. However, he was far from being recognised outside the German cultural sphere and so his successful conducting engagements in England were all the more emphatically acknowledged by Czech musical experts. His biographer Šourek summarised their importance when he compared them with the fate of Czech music in general: '. . . the music of a people of whose existence the inhabitants of Albion may not even have been aware! Can anyone challenge the great artistic and cultural significance of Dvořák's success?'[35]

Even in such exaggerations there was a seed of truth, though knowledge of the Czech people's existence did

Dvořák and his wife Anna photographed in London 1885

The Philharmonic Society was founded in 1813 by J B Cramer, P A Corri and W Dance to encourage professional performances of instrumental, chamber and orchestral music. In its first season a veritable who's who of the European musical elite were featured, including Clementi, Salomon, Viotti and Thomas Attwood. It was at one of its concerts in 1820 that Ludwig Spohr first innovated the use of a baton to conduct an orchestra and a few years later the Society commissioned Beethoven's Ninth Symphony. It continued to promote and support new music and composers. In 1869, they introduced analytical programme notes, indicating new expectations of audiences and a new educational openness very much in the spirit of their times. Dvořák always relished performing in England and wrote of the . . . *truly English enthusiasm, the like of which I have not enjoyed for a long while.*

not actually depend on even such a brilliant representative of its music as Dvořák. When he first aroused the enthusiasm of the English, he was so totally unknown to the music critics that they had to find out about him from German sources. When he left the island after his fifth visit he had truly won them over – at least those who were interested in contemporary music – and his fame in England competed with that of Brahms. (He was dubbed the 'Bohemian Brahms' – an honour indeed.) For Dvořák's compatriots, who reacted from the perspective of the mounting German–Czech nationalistic struggle with increasing sensitivity about their centuries-old dependence on all things German, his splendid reception by the distant Britons, whom they viewed with modest respect,

was more than a musical event. It represented international sanction of their national identity outside the confines of the Austro-German tradition.

A few years later, when Dvořák was in demand in America as a great master and Smetana was finally posthumously ranked as a genius (once the arrogant Viennese who despised the Czechs had enthusiastically hailed their discovery of *The Bartered Bride*), there was no further need of such self-glorification. In 1884, however, it caused a sensation when the Philharmonic Society invited a Czech composer to conduct his own works in London. No one had ever issued such an invitation to Smetana, who was much more famous in his own country.

Victorian England was at the peak of its world renown and in the 1880s could offer outstanding cultural attractions. Since Purcell, the great master of baroque music, England had not produced any composer of truly international standing, but through its wealth had given many European composers from Handel to Mendelssohn (and not only the geniuses) the opportunity to develop their art. The choral tradition fostered by Handel, an adoptive Englishman, was still flourishing in the 1880s. Nowhere outside Germany were there so many massive, ambitious choirs as in England.

The leading German conductor in England, Hans Richter, and the Joachim Quartet had prepared the ground well for the unknown Bohemian (the term in current English usage was applied to both gypsies and Czechs). The Philharmonic Society had already successfully performed the Slavonic Dances and the Slavonic Rhapsodies under Richter and in a typically English desire for personal contact they invited the unknown originator of these beautiful sounds to conduct his own works – preferably new ones.

Hans Richter (1843–1916) became principal conductor of the Vienna Court Opera in 1875 and also conducted the Vienna Philharmonic Orchestra from 1875–97. Having worked as von Bülow's chorus master at the Munich Opera, he conducted the Bayreuth premiere of Wagner's Ring Cycle in 1876. Upon leaving the Vienna Philharmonic he took over the reins of the Hallé Orchestra in Manchester, and also conducted the London Symphony Orchestra from 1904–11. He was an early champion of the works of Sir Edward Elgar.

In 1883 Sir Joseph Barnby had conducted Dvořák's *Stabat Mater* in London to unanimous acclaim (though strangely the Prague critics barely noticed; England was just too far away). In March

1884 Dvořák appeared in person on the other side of the Channel, accompanied by the pianist and court composer to the Fürstenbergs, Jindřich Kaan (only much later would he make the journey alone); to be warmly greeted in Dover by a fellow Czech, the military bandmaster L J Zavrtal, who was working in England, and in London by Henry Littleton, head of the music publishers Novello, in whose splendid house in Sydenham Dvořák stayed on his subsequent visits to London. This time, he stayed with the German pianist Oskar Beringer, whom Dvořák described as a *model of a musician, a real gentleman, who took complete charge of me.* The success of the *Stabat Mater* in the massive arena of the Royal Albert Hall was all the more sensational because he was even less known as a conductor than as a composer. *The Times* referred to a 'perfect interpretation' by an obviously experienced conductor and the *Morning Post* praised Dvořák's 'calm, unostentatious yet firm manner' of conducting. He could certainly not be described as a virtuoso conductor and later said grimly that he so often had to 'gesticulate' with his right hand when he would rather have been laying about him with it . . .

The metropolis of London and his reception there were an overwhelming experience for Dvořák. He wrote to his father in Kladno: *To give you a little hint of what London looks like and how enormous it is, just imagine to yourself: if you put together all the Czechs in the whole of Bohemia there would still be fewer of them than live in London! And if all the people of Kladno came into the huge hall where I conducted my* Stabat Mater, *there would still be room for them, because this Albert Hall is so colossal!*[36] He wrote home to his friend Karel Bendl: *Imagine the Neustädter Theatre about five times bigger and you will understand what the Albert Hall is like, where 10,000 people heard the* Stabat Mater *and 1050 musicians and singers played and sang and then there was this enormous organ!*[37]

In the same letter to his father we find that pride is, typically, closely followed by humble gratitude: *I cannot tell you how these*

An illustration of the Royal Albert Hall shortly after its completion

English people honour and love me! Everywhere they are writing and talking about me and saying I am the lion of this year's London musical season! . . . In some newspapers they wrote about you, too, saying that I came from a poor family, that my father was a butcher and innkeeper in Nelahozeves and that he did everything he could to give his son a proper education! All honour to you for that![38]

Two further concerts, including the D major Symphony, were equally successful; there were banquets, invitations and, most importantly, commissions. This time the Prague press reported fully and proudly the triumph of their fellow countryman and he was heaped with honours, but still the rivalry between the Smetana and Dvořák factions cast a shadow over his glorious homecoming. František Pivoda, who as a music critic was to Smetana as Hanslick was to Wagner and Bruckner, had called for a public reception for Dvořák at the railway station in Prague and as a result the musical delegation from the Artistic Association stayed away. This moment of Dvořák's greatest fame coincided with Smetana's tragic decline. A few weeks later he had to be admitted to the regional lunatic asylum in Prague and died there in May, while Dvořák was in Vysoká, enjoying domestic contentment, communion with nature and confirmation of his creative ability.

Out of the 3500 marks which Simrock paid him for the *Hussite Overture* and the piano cycle for four hands *From the Bohemian Forest (Ze Šumavy)* and the profits from his first visit to England, Dvořák had been able to fulfil one of his dearest wishes: he bought from his brother-in-law Count Kaunitz an old sheep barn in Vysoká and had it converted into a comfortable, single-storey country house large enough for his growing family. Here, near the nature he loved, he had a quiet study with a piano. From spring to autumn every year thereafter he took refuge from Prague in this mining village in the gently rolling countryside around Příbram, where quiet woods with their marshy pools made him feel at home. He liked sitting with the villagers in the inn and made friends with many of them, including the magistrate Antonín Rus from nearby Mirovice. He also loved working in the garden and bred doves. His letters from this first period at Vysoká exude deep contentment and pride in owning his own home, whether he was writing about his delight in a sunny day or reporting humorously to Simrock: *that in our family there is another new opus (a baby boy)! So you see, a new symphony and a little boy as well! What do you think about this creative force?*[39]

The symphony in question was his Seventh in D minor, commissioned by the Philharmonic Society in London. The fact that it and the oratorio *St Ludmila* owe their existence to the contacts he made in Britain was more important than his personal success as composer and conductor there, although that heightened his fame and so increased his value to his publishers as composer and collaborator. Simrock discovered this when he offered a mere

3000 marks for the D minor Symphony and found himself up against a stone wall, Dvořák having until then been very modest. *If I give you the symphony for M3000, I shall have lost about M3000, because other firms have offered me the sum* [meaning 6000 marks] *for it . . . to write no symphony, no major vocal works and no instrumental music and to publish perhaps a few songs here and there, piano pieces or dances or whatever: as an artist who wants to make his mark I can't do it! Now look, dear friend, that is how I see it from my artistic point of view . . . Please, remember that I am a poor artist and a family man . . .*[40]

WILLS'S CIGARETTES

PHOTO BY MASON

DVOŘÁK

Dvořák's fame in England saw him portrayed on cigarette cards

Dvořák got his 6000 marks but it was a long time since he had been a 'poor artist'. The English paid handsomely and fêted him at the Three Choirs Festival on his second visit in the autumn of 1884 where his *Stabat Mater* was given again. When he came back with new works: in April 1885 the D minor Symphony in London, in August *The Spectre's Bride (Svatební košile)* at the Birmingham Festival and in October 1886 *St Ludmila* at the Leeds Music Festival (the last two performed with huge choirs – 500 in Birmingham, 350 in Leeds), there were ovations everywhere and highly favourable reviews, which raved about the new symphony and declared it equal to anything by Brahms.

In his euphoria over all this good fortune Dvořák called *The Spectre's Bride* a composition *which surpasses all my previous work*, but this actually applies much more to the symphony and the oratorio. The English had asked him for a choral cantata and after long hesitation he had chosen a ghost story in ballad form by Karel Jaromír Erben (1811–1870). The story – of a bride carried off to the graveyard by her dead lover – can be found in the popular poetry of half of Europe, from Serbia through Russia to Scotland, and was also the source of Gottfried August Bürger's poem *Lenore*. In Dvořák's less harsh version a fervent prayer exorcises the ghost. The Czech title literally means *The Wedding Shirt*, but the English priest who translated it must have thought this unseemly and chose *The Spectre's Bride*. The main theme in A minor forms a bridge between the seven sections of this cantata for chorus, soloists and orchestra. Dvořák emphasises the lyric element over the dramatic which, together with the difficulties in portraying such a subject to a modern audience, diminishes its impact.

The larger *St Ludmila* is more important as it is the first great oratorio in the Czech language. Its wealth of brilliant choruses and lyrical solos for the protagonist recall the opera *Dimitrij*, though this time Dvořák had chosen a more patriotic subject (he had even briefly considered a text which paid homage to Hussite religious fanaticism). It is typical of his lack of literary judgement (he only thought of the musical opportunities) that he decided on the Christian story in which Czech patriotism takes second place. Jaroslav Vrchlický (1853–1912), who wrote it for him, was a well-known epic and lyric poet, a translator, essayist and highly cultured man and obsessed with rhyme. The flowery, long-winded and garrulous poetry in which he tells of the 9th-century conversion of Princess Ludmila and her betrothal to Duke Bořivoj, who had also been baptised, produced musical verses and numbers but hardly amounted to a thrilling narrative.

The English, accustomed to large choral set pieces, greeted this three-and-a-half-hour work in its English translation with enthusiasm but Dvořák, trying to turn it into a practical version for the theatre, attacked the score viciously with his red pencil. Freed from the hindrances of repetition and long-windedness, the oratorio was a great success in 20th-century Germany. The fugal cho-ruses demonstrate Dvořák's mastery of monumentalism and are unmistakably modelled on Handel.

Undoubtedly the D minor Symphony was the outstanding and most valuable result of the visits to England. After the premiere by the Philharmonic Orchestra under the composer's baton in St James's Hall in April 1885, subsequent performances under Hans Richter, Hans von Bülow and Arthur Nikisch spread Dvořák's international fame as a symphonic composer as far as Boston. That its model was Brahms's Third Symphony in F major, which the composer played through on the piano to his friend from Prague, is clear from its musical language, but its character is essentially Czech.

The minor key, symbolic for Dvořák, announces its basically militant character. The lines of motifs point to the *Hussite Overture* and anyone questioning its Czech national characteristics – as often happens – would have to ignore the 'furiant' character of the scherzo. This movement represents a return to Beethoven's sym-phonic style but in Dvořák's own musical idiom, though admit-tedly no programme offers us a key to how to assess it precisely. The composer himself said: *Just today I have finished the andante of my new symphony and I was as blissful and happy in this work as I have always been and may God grant that I shall go on like this, for my motto is and always will be: God, Love, Fatherland! And that alone will lead one happily to one's goal!*[41] Even this three fold motto is in fact a sort of programme, though a completely non-literary one, which unfolds in the prayer of the profound andante, the passion of the cantabile themes and the dramatic optimism of the whole concept.

The composition of the second series of Slavonic Dances, which Dvořák did not want to orchestrate in spite of Simrock's asking him to do so, completed the rich artistic harvest of these years. Among minor works, the four songs *In Folk Tone (V národnim tónu)* deserve mention as evidence of his ability to sublimate folk music, and together with the two Czech folk poems set spontaneously in Sydenham to a German translation they form a charming little series of original Dvořák folk songs. In November 1884 he conducted the *Hussite Overture* with the Berlin Philharmonic in Berlin, where it was greeted with greater applause than was the piano concerto, played by Anna Grosser-Rilke (an aunt of the poet Rainer Maria Rilke). He was conducting for the first time in Germany and this performance confirmed the fame of 'Anton Dvořák' as both composer and conductor. In spite of acrimonious correspondence with Simrock he was still unable to get his name spelt correctly on the music or in the programmes.

The triumphs in England and the works he wrote in these years formed the first high point of his life. Success and his newfound wealth suited him, but neither diverted him from his path towards personal and artistic self-realisation. When a Czech choirmaster wrote him a flattering letter, he replied: *I must honestly admit to you that your valued words have somewhat disconcerted me, because their obsequious devotion and humility read as though you were addressing a sort of demigod, which I never considered myself, do not consider myself now and never will. I am a simple Czech musician who does not like such exaggerated humility and although I have moved well enough into the great world of music, I am still what I was – a simple Czech jobbing composer . . .*[42]

Master and Teacher 1889–1892

In the summer of 1889 Dvořák wrote to his old friend Göbl: *You want to know what I am doing? My head is full and if only I could write it down all at once! But it's no use, I have to go slowly, at the speed my hand can move and the Lord God will do the rest . . . It is going more easily than I expected and tunes are just flying towards me . . .*[43] This evidence of the delight he took in composing is characteristic of the whole period he spent at home between his visits to England and his time in America. These years produced *The Jacobin* (*Jacobín*), the G major Symphony, the Requiem and the 'Dumky' Trio – all of which reached new heights in their respective genres and won for their composer honours and a teaching post. He had now come to his full stature and maturity and for the first time he could review his achievements while writing prolifically.

Conscious of his status and responsibility Dvořák now gave himself time to compose and took a whole year over *The Jacobin* (an exceptionally long period for him). His relationship with his main publisher Simrock reflects this new assurance. No longer was he a humble artisan writing to Simrock after an argument over consigning the D minor Symphony to England: *You seem to have a marvellous logic: I should compose and offer works to you – and*

The German publishing house of Simrock was founded in Bonn in 1790 by Nikolaus Simrock (1752–1834), a horn player in the electoral orchestra. The first of Beethoven's works to appear under this imprint was the Sonata Op 47 'Kreutzer'. The Berlin house was founded by Nikolaus Simrock's grandson, Fritz August (1838–1901) and was closely associated with the music of Brahms. In 1877 Brahms wrote to him about Dvořák: 'He is a very talented man. Besides, he is poor. Please take this into consideration.'

you simply refuse them! . . . No, I will not be taken for an idiot! And if you start threatening me, my demands will be considerably higher . . .[44]
Dvořák was angry that Simrock was only asking him for easy little pieces and Simrock complained – with justification – that the composer was offering his new works to other publishers in breach of the terms of his contract. This quarrel took three years to settle.

Previously Dvořák had sold several of his older compositions to his German publisher (*I have still have so many in my old trunk . . .*) and now began to bring them out, saying there was no reason for these works to be lost, seeing that he had written them with as much dedication then as he did now that he was famous. He revised his Symphonic Variations, his first symphonies and the *Cypresses* and devoted himself to reviving *The King and Charcoal Burner*, but the National Theatre's production of it was slapdash and once again it was a failure. Behind all this rummaging (*I like looking up my old sins*) lay an urge to improve on old compositions in the light of his new proficiency, rather than any slackening in his vitality.

The most unlikely circumstances sufficed to unleash his prolific creativity. On one occasion he was playing his viola with two amateur friends, and when the violinist found himself in difficulties technically Dvořák quickly wrote not one but two new, easier trios for two violins and viola. Once again practical in exploiting his inventions, he rearranged the second one as the four Romantic Pieces for violin and piano. When a long search in his trunk failed to turn up the manuscript of his early Piano Quintet, instead of continuing to look for it he wrote another, also in A major, which as op 81 was a masterpiece and a jewel of its kind. The flowing cantabile of the main theme of the first movement, introduced by the cello, could count as a 'calling card' for all his chamber music. The Quintet's emphatically Czech characteristics also marked the start of another Slavonic period for Dvořák: he named the second movement 'Dumka' – a Ukrainian musical form which changes abruptly between slow and fast tempi, meditation and action – and having meanwhile composed the vigorous, virtuoso Piano Quartet in E-flat, took it as the inspiration for the theme of his famed 'Dumky' Trio op 90 for piano, violin and cello. This Trio is in every respect an original piece of chamber music, written in six movements which diverge from the traditional Viennese sonata structure in new directions – for instance, the first three movements follow each other without a pause, something we also find in modified form in the G major Symphony.

All his theatrical disappointments to date could not thwart Dvořák's ambition to compose operas. In 1881 he had already been offered a libretto which he put on one side, but when he finally decided to set it to music the old enthusiasm seized him again. *I think the doubters will be happy with my dramatic talents this time and even surprised! As* The Spectre's Bride *and* Saint Ludmila *are the first of my new works (outside the theatre), I think* The Jacobin *will be my first opera.*[45] This prophecy was to be fulfilled, for *The Jacobin* was in fact his most inspired and successful work for the opera stage, after the later *Rusalka*, which was of quite a different kind. Another of his

A Dumka is a heroic ballad or poem, in origin specifically Ukrainian and usually meditative, often gloomy. In instrumental music, it tends to feature abrupt changes of tempo and mood swings – which are particularly apparent in Dvořák's innovatory op 90 Piano Trio; in fact these polarities provide the formal structure around which this work is built.

prophecies which came true was that because of its subject the opera would be *excellent for our home circumstances* but *not for the world at large.* After the premiere at the National Theatre in 1889 and the composer's later revisions, *The Jacobin* did enter the standard Czech repertoire but to this day is a stranger abroad.[46]

There is no valid reason for this. In *The Jacobin* Dvořák's dramatic talent could unfold in spontaneous, warm-hearted and

A view of the National Theatre in Prague by Viktor Maly, Dvořák's opera *The Jacobin* was first performed here in 1889

genuine musicality as never before, because Marie Červinková-Riegrová's libretto, based on a story by Alois Jirásek, was unsophisticated, though thoroughly stage-worthy (after some revisions, especially to the third act), and struck the most responsive chord in Dvořák's feeling for instrumentation. The protagonist is the village cantor Benda who approves of anyone who makes good music. He is a little vain (what obscure artist wouldn't be?) but his humanity bridges the social gulf between castle and village when it is a matter of playing the violin, cello or organ. This sympathetic figure is Dvořák's musical memorial to his German teacher Liehmann and to the hundreds of Bohemian cantors who through their music-making carried the banner of Czech culture in feudal villages and small towns during the centuries of its suppression. Liehmann's daughter, with whom the young Dvořák had enjoyed singing duets, was called Terynka, as was Benda's daughter in the opera, and to this character he gave his most magical folk tunes.

For the otherwise rather insipid eponymous character, the Count's liberal-minded son Bohuš, who is suspected of being a Jacobin, and his wife who comes from peasant stock, Dvořák reserved his most stirring tune *Music Alone*, which in eight bars of music straight from his heart was conceived – even by such a prolific melodist – in a moment of particularly dazzling inspiration. Bohuš is disinherited as a supposed Jacobin but eventually restored to his rightful heritage and two young lovers persecuted by the jealous castle steward are united in the end.

Jacobins are evil, but land-owning aristocrats are only so when they are cunning and deceitful and retribution quickly follows the treacherous Count Adolf. The lover Jiří performs a lively Slav dance and appears bold and rebellious, but only because he is anxious about his beloved, and the castle steward is rejected not as representing the upper classes but as a ridiculous old suitor. For Dvořák the feudal Bohemia of the late 18th century is a stable world, nostalgically transfigured by his youthful memories. The score contains many splendid numbers, such as the cantata rehearsal held by the village composer. The

Poster for *The Jacobin* 1889

naivety of the work still does not explain why, with all its musical superiority, *The Jacobin* did not even approach the international recognition accorded to *The Bartered Bride*. Most probably this is because the sentimental denouement, when the old Count is moved and softened by a lullaby, is difficult to make acceptable today, but this is the genuine Dvořák.

While he was working on *The Jacobin* Tchaikovsky, who was just one year older than Dvořák, came to Prague and he invited him to his apartment. They got on extremely well and their esteem was mutual. Tchaikovsky arranged for Dvořák to be invited to Russia and two years later, in March 1890, he went to Moscow and St Petersburg to conduct two concerts of his own works, including the F major Symphony. The public acclaimed him and Johannes Bartz, the director of the German Choral Society in Moscow, prepared the *Stabat Mater* in his guest's honour, but Dvořák was not happy with the Russian reviews. *These newspaper people don't care much about me – I could see that they were intriguing against me in Russian musical circles. You so-called Slav comradeship, where are you?*[47] Smetana had had the same experiences in Russia where *The Bartered Bride* was a failure.

Dvořák's success was less ambivalent in Germany, where he was cheered when he conducted in Dresden and Frankfurt, among other places, and where Hans von Bülow and Hans Richter were actively promoting his music. In England they never tired of asking for the maestro from distant Prague and in St James's Hall in London in April 1890 he conducted his new Symphony no 8 in G major, which had only just had its premiere in Prague, to the customary applause. One year later it won international acclaim under Hans Richter with the Vienna Philharmonic Orchestra. It is occasionally called the 'English' symphony, but this is purely because it was first published by Novello in London; it would be more correct to call it the 'Czech', at least in comparison with its predecessor in D minor which was modelled more on Brahms.

Dvořák wanted to make this work different from the 'usual, generally adopted and recognised forms'[48] and in fact this is the freest in form of his mature symphonies. The two outer movements are loosely connected through a similar main theme which dissects the G major triad. The first, with its abundance of themes, which are not analysed and elaborated at all, is like a vivacious, brightly coloured pictorial broadsheet and the finale combines variations with sonata form. Between them come a valse-scherzo and an adagio, which is redolent of the composer's profound joy in his natural surroundings at Vysoká and is the emotional point of repose of the whole composition.

This symphony's pictorial creation of a mood of joy is closely related to the thirteen piano pieces entitled *Poetic Tone Pictures (Poetické nálady)* which even have names like those of Schumann's *Waldszenen (Woodland Scenes)* – for example, *Nocturnal Path (Noční cestou/Nächtlicher Weg)* and *At an Old Castle (Na starém hradě/Auf einer alten Burg)*. It also resembles the three orchestral overtures which originally formed a cycle entitled *Nature, Life and Love (Příroda, život a láska)* but were later given individual titles: *In Nature's Realm (V přírodě)*, *Carnival (Karneval)* – which has a brilliant, bouncing syncopated main theme – and *Othello*, though the composer intended them to be played together. These constituted Dvořák's first foray into the programme music which he was to favour later in his life. They should be considered purely in musical terms, but in the composer's own words *they are still in a way programme music.*

The works which take their 'programme' from liturgical texts are more important among his compositions in this period. The Requiem is the apogee of Dvořák's sacred music and his other two religious compositions – the Mass in D major (his only mass) and the *Te Deum* – are so-called 'occasional' compositions. The Mass in D major was commissioned in 1887 by the wealthy architect Josef Hlávka for the dedication of a chapel in his castle near Plžen. Its charm lies in the simple vocal writing suitable for a country service with organ, though Dvořák later revised it for orchestra. The *Te Deum* (1892) commissioned for American Columbus Day celebrations, is more festive and equally fitted for its purpose as an oratorio, but the English text failed to materialise. Dvořák finally decided to choose one himself and considered the solemnity of the Latin *Te Deum* appropriate for such an occasion. The lapidary style of the four effectively contrasted sections, with soprano and baritone soloists and a mighty choral alleluia, remind one in places of Verdi and in others of Bruckner. When the English text for the cantata *The American Flag* by Joseph Rodman Drake (1795–1820) eventually arrived, Dvořák set it more out of a sense of duty than inspiration and the musical quality of his homage to the American flag as personifying the ideal of freedom is far inferior to that of the 'substitute' *Te Deum.*

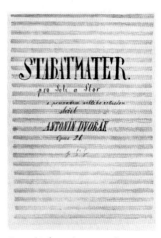

Dvořák's first title page of
Stabat Mater

The Requiem was written without any direct incentive, apart from a wish by the English for some kind of new oratorio, and unlike the *Stabat Mater* its music does not serve to sublimate a personal experience. He composed it during a period of repeated successes and untroubled contentment, of which the most radiant manifestation was his G major Symphony which immediately preceded it. That Dvořák could create a masterpiece of this kind out of the mass for the dead bears witness to his penetrating imagination and artistic concentration. He divided the liturgical text into two main sections and thirteen numbers. Chorus and soloists interweave in constantly changing combinations; one number, the *Recordare*, is sung by the solo quartet alone but it is the chorus which acts as the primary conduit for Dvořák's musical thoughts about the Last Things. In contrast to the *Stabat Mater* the musical language is colourfully personal and the working of the material and the orchestral palette show greater maturity. The introductory semitone theme is varied repeatedly and returns as the solemn final passage. It seems to be an objective reversal of the time-honoured B-A-C-H formula, but Dvořák's boundless power to wring emotion and typical Czech melody even out of the stony Latin text is overwhelming, and he based the choral fugue *Quam olim Abrahae* on a medieval Czech song 'Let us sing with joy'. If one compares Dvořák's Requiem with those of Mozart and Verdi, it stands closer to the former, because the operatic element, virtuoso solos and to a degree the dramatic impact of the *Dies Irae* are all subordinated to an intensely intimate lyricism. The composer conducted the brilliant world premiere in 1891 at the Birmingham Festival.

Dvořák on the day of his honorary doctor's degree from Cambridge University, June 1891

Honours were heaped upon him: the Emperor awarded him the Order of the Iron Crown, Third Class, which he received at a formal audience in Vienna; he was appointed Member of the Prague Academy of Science and both the Czech University in Prague and Cambridge University conferred on him honorary doctorates. In 1891 he returned to England for the ceremony and instead of making the traditional Latin speech he acknowledged this award in his own language, by conducting a performance of his G major Symphony.

Meanwhile a School of Composition had been set up within the

Prague Conservatory, which had been amalgamated with the old Organ School. The Director, Dr Josef Tragy, at first acted as head of the School of Composition but soon invited Dvořák to take his place. *Me a professor? Leave me in peace. My duty is to write, you should understand that, and not to be a schoolmaster*[49] was his initial reaction, which he confirmed by sending an official refusal. Eventually he gave way and for nearly eleven years, from 1891 to 1901, he was teaching composition either in New York or in Prague.

Once he had finally made the decision to give up some of his freedom, he took his duties very seriously and taught the third-year advanced students musical form, composition and instrumentation. He was always a teacher for highly talented students; he had nothing to offer those of lesser ability. Among the twelve pupils in his first year were two great future composers – Josef Suk, who married his daughter Otilie and became his loving and much-loved son-in-law, and Oskar Nedbal, and in the following year they were joined by Vítězslav Novák. All three were to become important figures in 20th-century Czech music and jewels in the crown of Dvořák's school.

These students recorded first-hand accounts of their teacher's very original and personal teaching methods. Because of his enthusiasm his classes habitually overran, disrupting the whole timetable, but bureaucracy was relaxed to make allowances for this famous figure. According to

The violist Oskar Nedbal (1874–1930) studied composition with Dvořák and like his near-contemporary the composer Josef Suk, was a member of the famous Czech quartet which took the name 'Bohemian Quartet' after its first independent concert in 1892. It became synonymous with the resurgence of Czech music and was closely associated with that of Dvořák, Smetana, Suk, Fibich and Foerster, as well as giving pioneering performances of new music by composers from Schoenberg to Ravel. Nedbal, whose most acclaimed composition was a sonata for violin and piano (op 9), left the Quartet in 1906.

Nedbal he was 'On the one hand a comrade, on the other a god'. Be that as it may, his students loved him, even when his demands made them despair. 'Sometimes I want to weep, but we learn a lot,' sighed Suk. Josef Michl considered him 'a moody man who suffered, probably like every great spirit, from so-called "eternal discontent". For instance, if he liked a passage in our compositions his first reaction was enthusiastic, but subsequently he would change his mind and demand that we alter, improve or even abandon it and replace it with something else.'[50] Suk praised Dvořák's immense musical knowledge: 'Bach, Handel, Gluck, Mozart, Beethoven, Schubert, Berlioz, Wagner, Liszt – he knew the works of all of them, down to the smallest detail. He did not underestimate Italian music at all and did not share the contemporary opinion that it was "barrel-organ music". He did not overlook anything new, either; he studied Bruckner, was interested in Richard Strauss and was delighted when he found his pupils were searching for new and independent means of expression.'[51]

His teaching methods were certainly not drily academic. He once asked a student: 'What is Mozart?' No theoretical answers satisfied him and finally he pulled the student by the sleeve to the window, pointed upwards and said: *Now just look here: Mozart is sunshine!*[52] He said composing was 'out of little making a great deal, a very great deal', and even 'something new'. *The only genuine composer is the one who creates something original!*[53]

In 1891 Dvořák received a telegram from America, inviting him to transfer his teaching from Prague to New York. This was a sensational offer, the like of which no Czech had ever received before, and the conditions were irresistible: $15,000 for only eight months' teaching (over 30,000 guilders, while the Prague Conservatory paid him 1200 guilders a year) and ten concerts of his own works. He refused at first and then hesitated for a long time. The prospect of leaving his beloved Vysoká for a strange world did not attract him, but Mrs Jeanette M Thurber

(1852–1946), the millionairess founder of the New York National Conservatory, had set her heart on her foundation being graced by a great European musical authority. She would not take no for an answer and finally Dvořák signed a contract as director.

The Prague Conservatory gave him leave of absence, he said goodbye to his homeland with a tour through several small Bohemian towns and in mid-September 1892 he set off on the long journey to the USA with his wife, Otilie and Antonín (their other four children stayed behind with his mother-in-law) and the young Czech-American Josef Jan Kovařík, who had been a guest student at the Prague Conservatory and was recruited by Dvořák as their travelling companion and guide to the USA. So began a new, brief but creatively significant chapter in Dvořák's life.

In the New World 1892–1895

At the end of September 1892 the Dvořák family landed in New York from the Bremen North German Lloyd steamship *Saale*. Manhattan had not yet acquired its grandiose skyline and the few tall buildings at the southern end of Manhattan Island did not 'scrape the sky', but Dvořák found the Statue of Liberty and the crowd of ships in the harbour overwhelming – *this view is breathtaking*. He felt at home when a Czech delegation as well as the secretary of the Conservatory came to welcome him, but though many newspapers and journals paid tribute to him on his arrival, he let this unaccustomed press activity pass him by. After staying

The Bremen North German Lloyd steamship Saale which took the Dvořák family to New York in 1892

briefly in a hotel, he rented a five-room apartment in a three-storey house on East 17th Street opposite Stuyvesant Park and

only a few minutes away from the Conservatory, and there he lived all the time he was in America. Three mornings a week he taught composition to a class of eight students, several of whom were black, and on two afternoons he rehearsed the student orchestra. His administrative duties as director were mostly taken care of by a secretary.

The whole time he was in New York he enjoyed a comfortable and carefree life and he loved it from the very beginning. *And how could I not, seeing it is so beautiful and free here . . .* he was soon writing home.[54] The democratic lifestyle appealed to him, too. *What really pleases me is that in America no one makes any distinction between a man and a gentleman. Nobody uses the term 'Your honour'. The millionaire says 'sir' to his servant, who says the same back to him, although he knows he is talking to a millionaire! So they are both 'Sirs', never mind the millions!*[55] Here speaks the naivety of an instinctively democratic Central European brought up in a feudal, class-ridden society. He was impressed to find that concerts where tickets were exorbitantly expensive were repeated shortly afterwards at a much lower price for the poorer members of the public, and that talented students received grants which paid in full for their studies at the Conservatory.

Dvořák kept to his customary lifestyle while in New York. He got up at six o'clock, walked over to nearby Central Park or down to the harbour, always with someone else – usually Kovařík who shared the family apartment. (For some while Dvořák had suffered

Dvořák's house in East 17th Street New York City

from agoraphobia.) To his trainspotting he now added an obses-
sion with ocean-going liners. 'There was no ship we wouldn't have
boarded and looked over thoroughly. On such occasions he first
chatted with the captain, then with his assistants and so we soon
knew every ship and all the captains and officers by name',
reported Kovařík.[56] On principle he hardly ever went out after six
o'clock in the evening. He ignored musical social life, except for
the Philharmonic concerts, and only went to the Metropolitan
Opera twice in two and a half years! He refused invitations and
preferred to spend the evenings with his family, usually playing
cards.

Musical life in New York was at that time by far the richest in
the USA. The Metropolitan, which in Dvořák's time was only
presenting French, German and Italian opera, was the only theatre in that gigantic country to stage opera at all. While Italian
divas sang at the Met, German-born conductors and musicians
dominated the concert halls. The New York Philharmonic
Orchestra, led by Anton Seidl, competed with the New York

Fountain in Central Park, New York

Central Park, New York at the turn of the 19th century

An early 20th century view of New York – of 42nd Street and the City Library

Symphony Society founded by Leopold Damrosch, the Boston Symphony Orchestra regularly gave guest performances there and many choral societies sang oratorios. The repertoire was dominated by German classical and romantic music but several of Dvořák's works were already known in New York.

American composition had not yet developed into a distinctive national style; the best-known American composer, Edward Alexander MacDowell (1860–1908), was rooted in German romanticism. Mrs Thurber expected that Dvořák's participation would not only enhance the prestige of her own teaching establishment but also help to enrich American music. Performances of his works were enthusiastically acclaimed, including the *Te Deum* in Boston and the D major Symphony and the Requiem (under Nikisch) in New York, but soon after starting work teaching and conducting he found himself embroiled in a confrontation of opposing views over the future of American national music. While some swore by the creative potential of Native American and black music, MacDowell rejected this theory, although he had himself written an 'Indian Suite'. 'In spite of Dvořák's efforts to dress up American music in Negro clothing, it is my opinion that such foreign artistry should have no place in our music, if it is to be worthy of our free country.'[57] Dvořák, on the other hand, stated in an interview published in the *New York Herald* in May 1893: *I am now convinced that the future music of this country must be built on the foundations of the songs which are called Negro melodies. They must become the basis of a serious and original school of composition which should be established in the USA.*[58] In an open letter, printed shortly afterwards in the *New York Herald*, he repeated this argument, while leaving out any mention of the National Conservatory in such a way that the hand of the idealistic but very businesslike Mrs Thurber can be detected behind it. Be that as it may, this famous composer's recognition of national American music aroused great notice in the musical press and redoubled curiosity about his first American work, especially as it was called *From the New World*, words which Dvořák had written spontaneously on the last page of the score.

A full page review of Dvořák's *New World Symphony* in the *New York Herald* 1893

The world premiere by the New York Philharmonic Orchestra under Anton Seidl on 16 December 1893 in Carnegie Hall was an overwhelming triumph, the newpapers having already written extensively about it after the general rehearsal. Dvořák reported proudly to Simrock: *The success of the symphony on the 15th and 16th December was magnificent and the newspapers say that no composer has ever had such a triumph. I was in a box, the hall was filled with the best New York audience and the people applauded so much that I had to thank them*

from the box like a king (!?) à la Mascagni in Vienna (don't laugh!).
You know that I like to keep clear of such ovations but I had to do it and
to show myself![59] Not only did the musical world become aware
that an extraordinary event had taken place, but Dvořák became
so commercially popular that collars, ties and walking-sticks with
his name on them were put on sale.[60]

This Symphony in E minor *From the New World*, Dvořák's ninth
and last, became his most popular and most internationally successful. It unites and enhances the merits of its two predecessors
in a kind of synthesis, made up of the clarity of form of the
Seventh and the bubbling abundance of ideas of the Eighth,
through thematically interweaving all its movements (it was new
for Dvořák to do so with such consistency) and giving the special,
quite novel 'American hue' to the themes. Not that he had in reality betrayed his own style and founded American national music;
the critics at the premiere already realised that. Leopold
Damrosch's verdict was: 'I cannot say whether or not this symphony is American. I see nothing American in it. It is Dvořák.'
The composer himself said: *That is and always will be Czech music.*

This is undeniable (how can one overlook the idealised liturgical dance in the trio of the scherzo?) but on the other hand
Dvořák's intellectual ownership of the 'American' themes was not
appreciated for a long time. Certainly there are allusions in every
movement: for example, the G major theme of the first movement
recalls the spiritual *Swing low, sweet chariot* but it is entirely
Dvořák's own invention. Even before the first performance he was
defending himself against any such insinuations: *It is the spirit of*
Negro and Indian melodies which I was striving to reproduce in my new
symphony. I have not used a single one of them; I have simply written
characteristic themes, imbuing them with traits of Indian music and
while using these themes as my raw material, I developed them with the
help of all the modern devices of rhythm, harmonisation, counterpoint and
orchestral colouring.[61]

A Dvořák family photograph taken shortly after their arrival in the United States in 1892

This makes sense in so far as it clarifies the composer's intellectual ownership but less so in the strict context of folklore. At the time Dvořák was not familiar with Native American folk music and it is doubtful whether the two street musicians whom (according to Kovařík) he later listened to with fascination in Spillville really had unadulterated folk music to offer. He would certainly have been better acquainted with Negro melodies through his black students, especially the intelligent baritone Henry Thacker Burleigh. What sounds American in this symphony is his intuitively creative adoption of ideas into his own musical language. In his earlier compositions there are plenty of forerunners of the pentatonic melodic structure so typical of most of the works he composed in America, which in fact is not a characteristic confined to Native American or black music but found in pre-tonal musical cultures from East Asia to Central Europe. Nevertheless one cannot ignore the fact that his experience in America contributed a new charm and colour to his music, including frequent use of the diminished seventh instead of the tonic, which adds a breath of exotic melancholy to the melodic development. He also added an American flavour to Bohemian syncopation, unmistakable in the long–short–long rhythm in the main theme of the first movement of this symphony. The harmonic boldness of the seven brilliant wind chords which introduce the largo is unusual for Dvořák and undoubtedly an echo of the overwhelming impression the New World made on him. Like Schiller, who created scenes of Swiss landscape in *Wilhelm Tell* without ever going to Switzerland, Dvořák's evocative imagination captured the breadth and grandeur of the American landscape in music before he knew the country at all, apart from one visit to Boston to conduct in the summer of 1893 after he had completed the score of the E-minor Symphony.

The church and school at Spillville in Iowa. The Czech colony where Dvořák composed the String Quartet in F major

Dvořák wanted to take his contractual home leave that summer but suddenly decided to accept an invitation from Kovařík to visit the Czech colony of Spillville in Iowa, where his father worked as a teacher and choirmaster. Essentially Dvořák the family man had to have all his loved ones with him. The other four children came over from Prague in the care of his elder sister Terezie Koutecká at the end of May and a few days later the party of eleven, including a maid, set off on the long journey to the Middle West.

Spillville had been founded a generation earlier by a Bavarian called Spielmann a few miles west of the upper Mississippi, halfway between Chicago and St Paul. A population of 350 farmers, mostly of Czech descent, lived in this settlement among fertile maize and potato fields, fruit plantations and woods. Dvořák felt at home in his rented single-storey stone house in this gentle landscape, among Czech-Americans who welcomed him like a king, though occasionally the isolation of the region depressed him. Spillville became his substitute Vysoká and he loved being among simple people with the children whom he had missed so much. The pastor of St Wenceslas Church drove him around in his carriage and they made music at home, Dvořák himself playing with an amateur quartet put together by Kovařík, because he was anxious to hear his first Spillville composition – the String Quartet in F major. This work was to become the most often performed of all his chamber music and a talisman for its composer. He only wrote quickly like this when his heart was full. In four days he had drafted all four movements and in fourteen had finished work on them, and yet this catchy 'American' quartet is most artfully constructed; the main themes of every movement are drawn out from the pentatonic core of the first one.

Out of the same contented mood sprang the Spillville String Quintet in E-flat major – more extensive and complex in the part-writing and emotionally more profound in the larghetto variation movement. Dvořák also took longer over its composition but he could not repeat the unique stroke of genius of the F major Quartet, which is reminiscent of the mystery of Mozart's and Schubert's creativity.

The months spent in the country passed all too quickly. On the way back Dvořák was acclaimed when he appeared to conduct a

festival concert on Czech National Day at the Chicago World Exhibition. He broke his journey for a day at Niagara Falls, which he described as overwhelming: *Heavens! That will be a symphony in B minor!* That key and the sketches he made in the five notebooks he filled during his stay in America indicate that his later Cello Concerto in B minor might have been inspired by the experience of Niagara.

In New York he went back conscientiously to his teaching. For Otilie and Toník he wrote the G major Sonatina for violin and piano which, despite its technical simplicity,

Portrait of Dvořák Conducting at the Chicago World fair of 1893 by V E Nadherny

is still an important work and a delight for amateur musicians. The 'Indian' larghetto in it reflects Dvořák's preoccupation with an American opera, which Mrs Thurber was persistently urging him to write. She put in front of him a libretto based on Longfellow's *Hiawatha*, the epic poem about a legendary Indian hero and Knight of the Grail, which he had read in Prague in a Czech translation and liked so much that it featured in the two middle movements of the E minor Symphony – the funeral and marriage from the Hiawatha Epic. However he got no further than drafting pentatonic themes in a notebook and when both this libretto and a new version were rejected by a committee Dvořák, always unsure about libretti, lost interest in pursuing it.

His relationship with opera at this time was definitely not a happy one. The 'golden horseshoe' of the Metropolitan seemed to him unsuited to his works – and rightly so. Verdi, Wagner and Rossini reigned there, sung by international, gold-plated larynxes, worlds away from Bohemian village cantors. Anton Seidl, with whom Dvořák had become close friends, invited him to a premiere of *Siegfried* at the Met. Dvořák went, but left his box after the first act. For all his respect for Wagner and for Seidl's conducting the insistent Nibelung rhythms got on his nerves. (He only went to the Met once again, to hear Rossini's *Semiramis*.) This did not prevent him from writing enthusiastically about his old idol: *What Wagner has done no one has done before him and no one will ever challenge! Music will go its own way, passing Wagner by, but he will stand firm like the statue of that poet from whom children still learn in school – Homer! Wagner will also be such a Homer!*[62]

One episode from Longfellow's 'Song of Hiawatha' was set to music in 1898 by the hugely popular black composer S. Coleridge-Taylor, and first performed in a student concert at the Royal College of Music, London. A complete setting was performed at the Royal Albert Hall two years later. Coleridge-Taylor, a pupil of Stanford, was heavily influenced by Dvořák's music. He travelled widely but lived and died in Croydon.

He took time from his teaching schedule in New York to write the five-movement Suite in A major, first for piano and later for orchestra, and the much more important Biblical Songs (Biblické písně) – ten songs for bass or alto solo and piano on Czech texts from the Book of Psalms – which represent the absolute peak of his vocal writing. The choice of his native tongue for a sacred work, unlike the *Stabat Mater* or the Requiem, indicates how personally involved he felt and the care with which he set the words confirms this. Possibly the death of his friend Tchaikovsky and his champion Hans von Bülow, or the news of his father's serious illness (he died a few weeks later) made him think seriously about mortality. He gave very personal expression to the biblical text and melodic outbursts spring from the words. The sublime spirituality of what is known as musicianship can be felt in Dvořák's ability to reveal a wealth of vocal variety, from terse declamation to flowing melody. One cannot help comparing this late work with Brahms's Four Serious Songs, but their deep scepticism is alien to Dvořák. Even when he is pleading 'out of the deep', his unshakeable faith glows through the bleak biblical landscape and it is no coincidence that the last of the songs which he decided were worth orchestrating (the remaining five were arranged later by other people), and also the final, tenth song, were hymns of praise to the greatness of God.

The following year he did spend his summer vacation in Bohemia and soon after the formal welcome by a delegation in Prague he hurried to Vysoká, where he produced the eight *Humoresques*, elaborations on sketches made in America. Number seven in G-flat major was a hit worldwide but tells us no more about his genius for inventing tunes than does his Piano Fantasy, which is more primitive than those of Chopin, Schumann and even Smetana. He wrote spontaneously for the keyboard but simply, to keep pace with his own fingers (he was no virtuoso), which should make his piano compositions easy for amateurs to play – 'should', because few of them are known outside Bohemia.

On his return journey to New York he stopped in Hamburg to visit the Czech composer Josef Bohuslav Foerster, who lived and worked there. He did not complete his third year in America. Because he was always homesick, he made Mrs Thurber's difficulties over payment (she owed him several months' salary to the end of his life) an excuse to break the contract on his side too, and travelled home to Prague in April 1895 before the end of the academic year. He never returned but bequeathed to America his Cello Concerto in B minor.

This was his best-known instrumental work, as American in its musical language as all the works he wrote in and under the influence of that country, yet as Czech as all his mature compositions. It surpassed the earlier concertos for piano and violin, both in substance and in its infinitely richer, high-romantic orchestration and deserved both the nickname 'Dvořák's Tenth Symphony' given to it by some Czech commentators and its popularity with both public and interpreters, including Pablo Casals. Not that any particular love for the cello led him to compose this work of genius for it; on the contrary, he thought it better suited to chamber music than to solo work (*at the top it snarls; at the bottom it growls*). He built its part into the symphonic flow and never used it to create virtuoso effects, but it is still the vehicle for some of his most sublime romantic and emotional ideas. He was now so sure of himself that, unlike with the earlier concertos, he vigorously resisted demands for technical alterations made by the cellist Hanuš Wihan, to whom it was dedicated. (Wihan founded the subsequently world-famous Bohemian String Quartet in which Dvořák's son-in-law Josef Suk played.) Instead – and this was another sign of his self-assurance – Dvořák gave the premiere to the English cellist Leo Stern, who visited Prague in 1895. Stern followed the composer's wishes unconditionally.

In Dvořák's two and a half years in America his works had soared to the heights of absolute masterpieces and brought more international fame to new Czech national music than to American. He had not been able to establish there a school equal to his Prague masterclasses nor to found an American national music – which in any case was not his intention. After he had returned home, the arguments over the future course of

American national music still raged and in 1903 Arthur Farell announced in a statement directed against MacDowell's European-style classicism, as though Dvořák's affection for folk-lore had never existed: 'We must immediately stop looking at everything through the mirror of German music, however wonderful and splendid this mirror may be. Then we must familiarise ourselves with modern Russian and French music . . .' and naturally with their own, American 'ragtime, Negro songs, Indian songs, cowboy songs . . .' Farell's foundation of the Wa-Wan Publishers for American music had certainly more effect than Dvořák's brilliant American creations on its autochthonous development.

For America, Dvořák's two and a half years there had 'roughly the same importance as the premiere of Mozart's *Marriage of Figaro* had for Prague', wrote Šourek in his biography of the composer.[63] For Dvořák himself the New York period was even more important and fruitful; to its stimulus he owed the awakening of creative powers which with a special, American flavour led him to the summit in his symphonies, chamber music and songs. Only in the field of opera were there still peaks to climb.

The Final Years 1895–1904

This time there was no ceremonial welcome in his homeland; Dvořák did not want one – only peace at Vysoká, the familiar rooms, the garden and his morning walks as dawn broke and the birds began to sing – everything which he had had to do without in New York. He was happy and as a result, lazy . . . *I rejoice in God's natural world and I am idle and do nothing. You may be surprised at this, but it is the truth, God's truth; I am a lazybones and am not touching my pen.*[64] At other times – as Kovařík, his companion in America, recalled – he fell into 'a bad mood as soon as he had nothing to do. He was then to a greater or lesser extent irritated or distraught, it was hard to talk to him, the most trifling question often made him angry, sometimes he answered but often not a word; he was always like that when he was collecting his thoughts for a new work. However, as soon as he had made up his mind about his next composition, his ideas were clear and he started writing, he

J J Kovarik, Dvořák's pupil who accompanied him to the United States

became a completely different person. Absorbed in his work he did not care whether the earth was rotating from east to west or the other way round. He worked quietly and contentedly, was happy when it was going well and when something, as he would say, was "successful", he was in the best of moods – truly charming, always smiling and joking.'[65]

This uncharacteristic laziness only lasted for a few months. By late autumn 1895, having resisted all Mrs Thurber's appeals to return to New York without any great qualms of conscience and having indicated that he was willing to resume his teaching at the Prague Conservatory, the urge to compose seized him again . . . *Thank God we are all well and glad after a three year absence to be able to celebrate the joyful Christmas holidays we love in Bohemia! . . . that is why we all feel so inexpressibly happy.*[66] The creative expression of the bliss his homeland brought him was the two String Quartets in G major and A-flat major (numbered in reverse order). Both occupy historically significant positions in Dvořák's work, the former being the more important, because of its first two movements. With them, these fruits of his being *inexpressibly happy*, he bade farewell to that absolute music which he had enriched so prodigally and with such pioneering originality in his own country. To the end of his life, eight and a half years later, he did not write another note of 'pure' (that is, symphonic or chamber) music, but only tone poems and operas, where words were involved.

This late turning-point could only have surprised those who sought to find a hidden meaning in the intellectual logic behind Dvořák's compositional process, which was in fact much more determined by fundamental motives, though they seem quite obvious. The turning towards 'symphonic poetry' did not come at all suddenly. Famous as he was in both continents as a symphonic composer, what made him turn in the direction of the so-called 'new Germans', that is, towards Liszt and Richard Strauss? We know that he had admired Liszt since his days as a viola player (*Only what Christ taught and Liszt wrote will endure through the ages*)[67] and his life long idolising of Wagner was never affected by his personal friendship with Brahms and Hanslick. As he studied

Strauss's early symphonic poems such as *Don Juan, Till Eulenspiegel* and *Tod und Verklärung (Death and Transfiguration)*, and as on his return from America he was again working intensively on Liszt and may even have suspected that it would be difficult for him to surpass a masterpiece like his Ninth Symphony, the move towards programme music is not so surprising. There are several examples among his previous works – the three orchestral overtures *In Nature's Realm, Carnival* and *Othello* and the cycle for four hands *From the Bohemian Forest* – but at the time he had only vaguely hinted at a poetic 'programme'.

Dvořák now wrote no less than five symphonic poems, one after the other, mostly in 1896, four of them – *The Water Goblin (Vodník), The Noon Day Witch (Polednice), The Golden Spinning Wheel (Zlatý Kolovrat)* and *The Wild Dove (Holoubek)* – based on Karel Jaromír Erben's collection of reproductions of folk poetry, entitled *Posy of Flowers (Kytice)*, which could be compared *mutatis*

Leos Janáček at his desk in 1904

mutandis with Herder's *Stimmen der Völker in Liedern (Voices of the People in Songs)* or *Des Knaben Wunderhorn.* In a letter to Hans Richter, whom he admired and respected with gratitude for pioneering his works, he wrote: *The pieces are more in folk idiom – sometimes the dramatic element comes out strongly. They are ballads and in each one there are three or four characters whom I have made an effort to personalise.*[68] These 'ballads' he refers to are the first three symphonic poems, composed quickly one after the other in early 1896. In them he was following Erben's ballads so exactly that the instruments often play a wordless setting of individual verses. In an analysis written after the first performance in Brno, Janáček acknowledged an affinity with his own theory of 'spoken melody' (*nápěvky*): 'They grow freely out of the same atmosphere as folk songs.' He saw in Dvořák's symphonic poems an inspired, fundamental connection with folk compositions and called them the 'most Czech of Dvořák's works'.[69]

It is strange that Dvořák wanted to set to music the horrific and bloody stories on which these three symphonic poems are based. *The Water Goblin* tells of a vengeful sea spirit who drags a girl down with him and gives her a child. When the girl leaves him he throws the head and body of the murdered child at her feet. In *The Noon Day Witch* a mother conjures up the witch to frighten her child who refuses to eat and she appears in earnest, to the mother's horror. The child dies. *The Golden Spinning Wheel,* which lasts half an hour – twice as long as any of the others – is a fairy tale of a king's son and a poor girl who is murdered by her stepmother to favour her own child, but through magic it all ends happily. Even Dvořák's artistry could not make such an unmusical subject plausible and friends like Suk, Richter and Janáček tried in vain to rescue it by making cuts. *The Wild Dove* is another macabre ballad: a woman has poisoned her husband and remarried. A dove, symbolising her guilty conscience, proclaims her misdeed and drives the woman to suicide. In its atmospheric density and skilful thematic variations, with almost all the motifs deriving from one nucleus, this is the best of these simple programme pieces, which cannot be compared with either Liszt's or Strauss's poems of ideas.

The musical treatment of the shorter pieces follows the more supple, ballad style of each poem. *The Water Goblin* is in free rondo form, with a typical Dvořák coda of reconciliation and mourning; the *Noon Day Witch* has four contrasting movements like a symphony and in the case of *The Wild Dove*, composed at the end of 1896, Dvořák even numbered the five sections of the score

Eduard Hanslick felt drawn to register a 'quiet, friendly warning' when he heard *The Water Goblin* and *The Noon Day Witch* performed under Richter in Vienna; he feared that Dvořák might clash with Strauss. Dvořák, however, does not seem to have thought that such a great misfortune, for in 1897 he added another symphonic poem, his last (nothing to do with Erben's collection), which does really remind one of Strauss, not only because it is called *Heroic Song (Píseň bohatýrská)* and Dvořák had originally intended to call it *A Hero's Life* (Strauss's *Ein Heldenleben* came out a year later). This title was apparently suggested to Dvořák by his pupil Vítězslav Novák but the composer never explained its programme. In character it is a variation on Beethoven's style, crowned with a somewhat bombastic apotheosis. Šourek defended this rarely performed work and thought it greatly undervalued, while even the arch-critic Mahler liked it: 'I have just received your second work *Heroic Song*, and am as enthusiastic about it as I was about the first one [referring to *The Wild Dove*].'[70] In fact Mahler successfully performed both works in Vienna and continued to show Dvořák his friendship and support.

More successes followed. The Bohemian String Quartet enjoyed fresh triumphs with the two recently composed String Quartets, especially in Germany, and its international reputation grew in the next years in step with that of Dvořák's works. At home he

The Bohemian (Czech) Quartet founded by Hans Wihan (violoncello) with Karl Hoffmann, Joseph Suk (second violin) and Oscar Nedbal (viola) photographed in 1897

was honoured on all sides. When in January 1896 after years of wrangling, the Czech Philharmonic Orchestra had finally been formed out of the National Theatre's opera orchestra; its first public concert was a programme of Dvořák's works performed under his baton.[71] His new works also benefited from his American fame; Simrock, who had paid him limited amounts for even his great symphonies, paid 12,000 marks for the first three symphonic poems.

Dvořák had quickly resumed his old lifestyle. He was again teaching industriously in the cramped rooms of the Conservatory in the Konvitská, although he never found intakes of such highly talented students as before, and again fleeing as soon as he could in late spring to his beloved Vysoká. Again his days revolved in a regular circle of home, railway station and his usual café table in the evenings, where he sat with his friends. To this routine was added Friday evenings in the house of Josef Hlávka, President of the Czech Academy of Sciences and Arts, where he could make music and talk with Czech intellectuals, such as the poets Julius Zeyer and Jaroslav Vrchlický, the politician Dr Rieger and the sculptor Josef Václav Myslbek, who had created the St Wenceslas Memorial in the square of that name. In the Pilsner Inn in the Myslíková the merry party of intellectuals calling themselves the 'Mahulíkovci' had got together again – a regular group of musicians who gathered around Novák and the Bohemian String Quartet and acknowledged Dvořák as their undisputed leader whenever he appeared. On the stroke of nine, however, he always left and not even the most lively discussion could keep this habitual early riser any later.

Dvořák stayed at home more and more. He liked paying short visits to friends in Bohemia more than travelling abroad, even in order to promote his fame as composer and conductor. Not even England could draw him any more. In March 1896 he went there for the ninth and last time to conduct the Eighth Symphony, the Cello Concerto and the Biblical Songs, but the wet weather and wretched food hastened his return home. Thereafter his only journeys were to Berlin, where in 1900 he heard his Ninth Symphony truly capture the hearts of the previously restrained audience in the imperial capital, to Budapest and several times to Vienna, which he did

Johannes Brahms

not like. This imperial capital also acclaimed him as a composer, above all thanks to Richter's influence as conductor of the Vienna Philharmonic Orchestra. Dvořák repeatedly visited Brahms, to thank him for his unselfish work in correcting his proofs while he was in America and finally, in March 1897, when his friend was seriously ill. Only a few weeks later he was back again, for the funeral of the fellow composer he most respected and admired.

On an earlier visit to Vienna, in March 1896, he had called on another great contemporary, Anton Bruckner, in his apartment in Schloss Belvedere Park. Josef Suk, who was with Dvořák, remembered: 'We found him sitting at his desk with no coat on, and had the impression that here lived a man who was entirely immersed in his intellect and his work . . . When we took our leave, he was suddenly very upset. There were tears in his remarkable eyes. He accompanied us to the door in his quilted waistcoat and waved kisses to us as long as our carriage was in sight . . .'[72] A few months later Bruckner was dead. The main explanation why

The organist and symphonist Anton Bruckner (1824–1896) might be best described as the composer who expressed the Wagnerian aesthetic symphonically – ironically, the medium which Wagner had famously declared dead. His relationship wth Brahms was complicated by this adulation, and the two never managed to repair their differences, even though they were both closely involved with the Conservatory in Vienna. Bruckner also suffered the opprobrium of Hanslick, and somewhat pathetically, upon receiving a decoration from the Emperor Franz Josef, implored him to silence the critic.

these two composers, who had in common so much that was fundamental to their work – deep Catholicism, simple creativity and an affinity with the popular origins of melody – never developed a personal relationship lies in the current divisions in musical politics, but one can still appreciate the differences between the natures of these two Wagnerians – the mystic and the music-maker.

Dvořák's peaceful, creative daily life in the last years of the century was marked by both sad and happy personal events. Soon after Brahms's death he had to take his leave of an even older friend, Karel Bendl, who had been his first helper and supporter. He felt deeply satisfied and honoured to be elected as Brahms's successor on the Viennese commission responsible for awarding the stipend which he himself had once received, thanks to Brahms, and in the following years he helped Vítězslav Novák and many other talented Czechs in the same way. His greatest joy of all was the celebration of the marriage of his daughter Otilie to Josef Suk, who had meanwhile become a prominent musician. At his wish the wedding took place on the same day in November 1898 as his own silver wedding. Although he had diplomatically refused a ministerial invitation to compose a ceremonial march for the Emperor Franz Joseph I's golden jubilee, he was awarded the title of 'Litteris et artibus' ('for letters and the arts'), but this was less important to him; he spoke disparagingly of it as the *big gold plate*.

Once again he was working on a new and grandiose opera score. In the previous ten years he had written no new operas but had thoroughly revised his last two, *The Jacobin* and *Dimitrij*. All his hopes of being as successful internationally on the stage as in the concert hall had been disappointed and yet on the brink of old age he

Poster for the premiere of Dvořák's opera *Dimitrij* in 1882

embarked on a new dramatic work and dedicated all his time from then on to opera. What led him to do this? He had several reasons, the most personally relevant definitely being that he felt he was an impassioned composer of operas who still had something to say, even though many people did not agree. Though normally taciturn over aesthetic matters, in an interview with the Vienna journal *Die Reichswehr* shortly before his death Dvořák spoke unusually fully about his relationship with opera. *In the last five years I have written nothing but operas. I want to dedicate all my strength to opera, so long as the good God still grants me health. Not in any way out of a desire for fame in the theatre, but because I believe that opera is the most suitable creation for the general public. This music attracts the widest audience and very often, too; when I compose a symphony, however, I might have to wait years before it is performed here. Simrock has asked me for chamber works, but I steadily refuse. My publishers now know that I shall not write anything more for them. People bombard me with questions why I do not write this, that or the other; I do not want to any more. I am regarded as a symphonic composer and yet many years ago I demonstrated my overwhelming inclination towards dramatic composition.*[73]

There is an element of sadness and bitterness in this. The sentence about his *overwhelming inclination* seems exaggerated in relation to his whole life's work, though it does actually apply to his last years. The sensational success of Smetana's *Bartered Bride* in

19th century illustration of a scene in Smetana's opera *The Bartered Bride*

Vienna and its triumphal progress through Europe must have stimulated Dvořák's ambition. In addition, with Wagner's breakthrough and Verdi's later works in the mid-1890s opera reached the summit of its popularity among the middle classes and younger Czech composers entered the scene at the Prague National Theatre: Fibich with *The Tempest (Bouře)* and *Hedy*, Foerster soon after with *Eva* and Karel Kovařovic with *The Dog Heads (Psohlavci)*, all of which are still popular with the Czech public. Janáček had already taken his first steps onto the opera stage and was working on his masterpiece *Jenůfa*.

In America Dvořák had discussed at length with the Wagnerian Anton Seidl the question of modern opera in the wake of Wagner's music dramas. He had resolved to embark on a new operatic venture. When his early symphonic works were performed in Vienna, several critics had detected dramatic characteristics in them. Ludwig Speidel called them 'dramas without a stage, music without singers' and said that an important new chapter in musical history should be written – 'Anton Dvořák and dramatic music'.[74] The composer followed with interest the Viennese reaction to his new genre of programme music and admitted that the reviews had influenced him, so when in the spring of 1898 František Adolf Šubert, then director of the National Theatre, offered him a libretto by his nephew Josef Wenig (1874–1940), Dvořák was extremely receptive. Wenig, a 24-year-old teacher, had quite skilfully dramatised in simple free verse a traditional Czech fairy tale about the stupid, gullible devil, on which Božena Němcová had already written a play which J K Tyl had staged. Wenig was no poet but he was an experienced translator of stage works, including *Die Fledermaus* and *Orpheus in the Underworld*. That his pedestrian and unpoetic style avoided pseudo-poetical flourishes and the repetition customary in opera is less to his detriment than his amateurish attempts at drama. Such inadequate partnerships were Dvořák's lifelong burden. It may be that the landmark international success of Humperdinck's *Hänsel und Gretel* enticed him to write a fairy-tale opera; in any case he was happy with the subject, as he had just become absorbed in Erben's fantastical folk ballads.

Čert a Káča – literally, *Kate and the Devil* – tells of a peasant girl with a fiery temper whom no one wants to dance with except the devil, who dances her away to hell. There no one is happy with the unruly girl and the good shepherd Jirka, who follows her down to the underworld, has no trouble in freeing her from the clutches of the devil whom she is tormenting. When the duchess (who appears without any reason in the third act!) is about to be carried off by the devil because of her harshness to her subjects, she only has to repent and the crafty Jirka beguiles the devil by threatening to bring Kate back to hell. This sounds very funny, and is, when Dvořák transforms hell into a Bohemian village inn, but his Wagnerian declamatory style sits awkwardly with the simple, warm-hearted, folk story. (Janáček used this style as an example of his theory of words and music, saying that Dvořák was 'following the melody of the Czech words.') There are few arias in the score but plenty of dance-like tunes. The nimble *parlando*, animated with leitmotif variations, shows the maturity of the composer's craft but his best quality – melodic inspiration – has less opportunity to unfold here than in earlier works. The opera was carefully staged and successfully premiered at the Prague National Theatre in November 1899.[75]

In contrast, such inspiration blossomed in *Rusalka*, which followed directly after *Kate and the Devil* and was Dvořák's dramatic masterpiece. 'When I wrote the libretto for *Rusalka* in the autumn of 1899, I had no idea that I was writing for Antonín Dvořák. I wrote without knowing who it was for . . .' wrote Jaroslav Kvapil (1868–1950),[76] who was definitely Dvořák's best poet-collaborator, though this does not mean that his *Rusalka* is a masterpiece of its kind; with all its pure poetic qualities, it lacks the theatrical thrust which distinguishes a simplistic libretto like that of Lortzing's *Undine*. More interesting than the fact that composers like Suk and Foerster had declined to set it to music, is that a young poet had written a libretto on the off-chance – a token of the prestige which attached to opera. Once again it was the theatre director Šubert who offered Dvořák the libretto and once again the composer jumped at it. He only needed to combine in creative imagination his childhood memories, imbued as they were with fairy-tale folklore, with the poetry of nature; the quiet pools full of whispered sounds in the countryside around his beloved home of Vysoká evoked his response.

The title page to the score of Dvořák's opera *Rusalka*

Dvořák spent almost the whole of 1900, from April to November, composing *Rusalka*. The story of the water nymph who lures humans down to their death in the depths had aroused the imagination of people in the west for centuries, as Ondine, Rusalka or Melusina. Heinrich Heine's Lorelei is the best known of the mythological sisters, who symbolise the mysterious and disturbing eruption of a personification of nature into the world of human beings. Kvapil's libretto relies freely on de la Motte-Fouqué's tale, but also shows the influence of Lortzing's *Undine* and Andersen's fairy tale *The Little Mermaid*, while some scenes and verses are taken from Gerhart Hauptmann's *Versunkene Glocke (Submerged Bell)*.

Rusalka is a water sprite who yearns to become mortal; the condition is that she will then remain silent. A prince woos her and a princess makes him leave her; Rusalka returns to her own element and the prince's remorse comes too late. Her kiss is now fatal. Kvapil's poem is full of *fin de siècle* pessimism: the natural beings are good-natured – the merman, Rusalka's friend and

Marie Mikhailova the Russian Soprano in the first performance of *Rusalka*

father-figure, appears here as a kind version of the water goblin in Dvořák's symphonic poem – while the humans are selfish and wicked. The composer's sympathies lay entirely with the natural creatures. The music of the prince and princess is merely conventional, while Rusalka and the creatures of her world enjoy his overflowing lyricism, not only in the most famous number in the score, the G-flat major Song to the Moon. The enlivening of the song forms and ariosi which simply follow the words, the wealth of leitmotifs, not just linked to individuals but also to psychological situations, the rich palette of harmony and orchestration, all reveal Dvořák the admirer of Wagner on a previously unsurpassed summit of mastery, without betraying his personal integrity and without sublimating the string of exquisite, opulent melodies into a musical drama. The subtitle 'Lyrical Scenes', which Tchaikovsky gave to *Eugene Onegin* as an indication of its genre, is more appropriate to the particular nature of *Rusalka*.

The composer worked hard and happily on the score . . . *I am full of enthusiasm and joy that the work is going so well!*[77] The premiere in the Prague National Theatre on 31 March 1901 was Dvořák's greatest operatic triumph yet and announced the birth of the second most popular Czech opera, though it comes an appropriate distance behind *The Bartered Bride*. Success abroad came slowly; only in 1908, after his death, did the first foreign theatre, in Ljubljana, show any interest and another 20 years went by before the first German-language performance, in the small North Bohemian town of Jablonec. However, after World War Two the lyrical glories of *Rusalka* began to be appreciated abroad, especially in Germany, and the novel 'impressionistic' sounds which Dvořák created in this his most mature score were quickly noticed. His French contemporaries Debussy and Ravel influenced him less than Richard Strauss, whose works, according to Suk, he was studying intensively at the time. Šourek speaks of a *Rusalka* impressionism 'which is not only expressed in a preference for the play of colours between half light and half shade but is also transformed through the power of Dvořák's artistically balanced personality into the expressive lines of that musically distinct Czech impressionism which unfolds later in the works of Vítězslav Novák and Josef Suk'.[78] Among the chorus of critics who were positive and enthusiastic about *Rusalka* was heard a sharply disparaging voice: 'As we cannot accept any other form of operetta than musical drama, the whole purpose behind *Rusalka* makes it a bad, faulty work.'[79] The voice, belonging to a critic called Zdeněk Nejedlý who was only 23 years old at the time, would not have been important had he not contributed so intransigently to the denigration of Dvořák as an opera composer when he later became the influential head of the Smetana party and then Minister of Culture in Communist Czechoslovakia.

Come on, quick, quick – any new libretto will do! called Dvořák cheerfully to his friend Kvapil when he saw him for the first time soon after the premiere, but Kvapil had nothing ready and in fact more than a year went by before Dvořák decided on a new and final opera. He entered into negotiations with Gustav Mahler, then Director of the Court Opera in Vienna, who wanted to perform *Rusalka* with Leo Slezak as the prince. Dvořák was offered a very generous contract, but just as the conditions for success at last in a great German-language theatre seemed more favourable than ever before, he incomprehensibly delayed so long before giving his consent that other repertory considerations thwarted Mahler's plan. However, La Scala in Milan rang to Dvořák's orchestral music, when Toscanini brilliantly conducted his Ninth Symphony. Dvořák's pupil Oskar Nedbal was promoting his music by conducting it all over Europe, as was Hans Richter with tireless enthusiasm, and the composer was especially happy when in April 1901 Arthur Nikisch visited Prague with the Berlin Philharmonic and after a performance of *The Wild Dove* directed the applause towards his box. The orchestra played a fanfare for him and he had to come down to the podium. Shortly before this he had received a great official honour when he, as the first ever composer, and Jaroslav Vrchlický, representing Czech literature, were nominated by the Emperor as members of the second house of the Austrian Parliament, the 'House of Lords'. Dvořák put on his tail-coat to take the oath (in Czech) in the senate, which consisted mainly of the nobility. His first appearance there was also his last. Verdi had held the same view on politics. Every member of the Austrian Parliament had a desk with a drawer in front of him, an inkwell, a sand-shaker, blotting-paper, pens and a few sharpened pencils, Hardtmuth no 2, which were soft, yet firm, the best product of their kind. Dvořák liked these pencils very much. He put them all in his pocket. When he left the parliament building he showed them to his wife who was waiting for him and said: *Look at these, they're just the thing for writing music!*[80]

But he did not compose for a long time, apart from the incidental Festival Song (Slavostní zpěv) for the 70th birthday of the former Conservatory director Dr Josef Tragy. The current director, Bennewitz, was now also retiring, so who should succeed him but the most celebrated composer among the professors? In July 1901 Dvořák was elected as director of the institute but it was agreed that this should only be a ceremonial post. The management was handled by the efficient Karel Knittl and everyone was happy to have Dvořák still teaching composition there. His 60th birthday was suitably celebrated. His birthplace Nelahozeves honoured its most famous son in a festival with a mass, speeches, banners and a salute of guns – but in the absence of the object of these festivities, who had fled from them all to Vienna, just as Prague was mounting a cycle of his works at the National Theatre with many of his operas more or less carefully staged: *The Stubborn Lovers* (paired with a ballet based on one of the Slavonic Dances), *The Cunning Peasant, Dimitrij, The Jacobin, Kate and the Devil, Rusalka* and finally a staged performance of the oratorio *St Ludmila.* This was a lavish operatic celebration of his birthday, though not the complete cycle of his stage works which had been originally planned.

In November the shy object of these celebrations finally had to appear at the postponed official birthday party. As the torchlight procession from the National Theatre reached his house in the Korntorgasse, voices called to him repeatedly to come to the window (*Tell them to stop this shouting!*) and then down into the courtyard, among all the party-goers. He thanked them, saying that all his life his motto had been *Through song to the heart, through the heart to the homeland* and so it would always be.[81] In many towns all over Bohemia and Moravia, the Czech people celebrated his birthday in the same nationalistic spirit as in Prague.

Around that time Edvard Grieg, with whom Dvořák was on friendly terms, came to visit him in Prague, but life was not all pleasure. Friends and colleagues had died – Zdeněk Fibich, hailed as Smetana's successor, in 1900 at the age of only 50, a year later Verdi and Fritz Simrock, for many years his comrade and the herald of his fame, who died in Lausanne after a long and painful illness. Was Dvořák in tragic mood, when he finally, after an unusually long period of idleness, decided to collaborate again with Vrchlický, the librettist of *St Ludmila*, by setting to music his libretto for *Armida*, which had lain on the composer's desk since 1888? (. . . *I have not worked for more than 14 months, I can't start on anything and I don't know how long this situation will last.*)[82] It had already been offered to Karel Kovařovic, composer and chief conductor of the National Theatre, who showed a better instinct for music drama than Dvořák when he gave up sketching out music to it.

If there was ever an impossible libretto (and there are certainly plenty of those), then this was it. Dvořák immediately fell prey to Vrchlický's hypocrisy, probably enticed by the chance that a story from world literature might give him to win over the German and international opera houses who had shown no interest whatever in his Bohemian and Slav material.

The story of *Armida* originated in Torquato Tasso's *Gerusalemme liberata* and had been repeatedly set as an opera in the past – by Lully, Handel, Gluck and Rossini among others. Vrchlický elaborated the love story of the crusader Rinaldo and the beautiful pagan Armida with a Christian and humanistic ethos, which appealed to Dvořák's religious instincts. In his reverence for Wagner he was also fascinated by the fact that the theme of seduction and redemption had its parallel in *Tannhäuser*, which he regarded as Wagner's greatest work. However Vrchlický's libretto faded into routine rhyming verse, failed in its psychological definition of the characters and sought refuge in weakly motivated supernatural effects reminiscent of long outdated stagecraft. The score is undoubtedly better than the opera as a whole. Even though the age of chivalry is symbolised by somewhat hollow sentiments which imitate Wagner only in their declamatory style, and its opponent Ismen appears as a mere operatic intriguer and villain. Dvořák is inspired by emotion and pity rather than by heroics, as in the lyrical representation of the eponymous heroine or in the warmth of the G-flat final duet, he rises in this his last opera, which in essence was alien to his nature, to the highest peak of his creative powers.[83]

At the premiere in March 1904 the public paid loyal tribute to their beloved and venerated maestro. He was unhappy about the production. It had had to be postponed because of a strike by the orchestra against Kovařovic, and the staging suffered from inadequate decor. The composer participated actively in the rehearsals but was bad-tempered throughout.

Dvořák himself thought *Armida* his best opera (even geniuses are not necessarily their own best judges). Meyerbeer's *Gli Ugonotti (The Huguenots),* for long a symbol of an old-fashioned, superseded type of opera, delighted him; *Carmen* he found musically magnificent, but immoral, which was what Beethoven thought about *Figaro* and *Cosí fan tutte*. In Puccini's *Tosca* he found fault with the parallel fifths, which just sounded wrong to his ears, schooled as they were in the pure four-part harmonies of Haydn, Mozart and Beethoven. However, this did not make him an academically fossilised teacher. He drew the attention of one of his former pupils 'with a serious face' to the 'false notes' in the piano score of Gustave Charpentier's new opera *Louise*: *Look here, my boy, this Charpentier is a strange musician. There are wrong notes everywhere! . . . So – how would you improve it?* When the pupil timidly made some suggestions, Dvořák looked at him 'with contempt', pointed to Charpentier's chord and declared: *No – he's got it right!*[84]

Immediately after completing *Armida*, Dvořák took up yet another libretto, which was probably even more impossible than that of *Armida* and certainly more amateurish. The industrialist Rudolf Stárek had based it on the old Czech saga of the hero Horymír who, mounting his horse, leaped from Vyšehrad into the Vltava, and Dvořák covered five pages with sketches for the score. However, during the premiere of *Armida* he was suddenly taken ill and had to leave his box. He had never been ill in his life but now for the first time he had to stay in bed and did not get up again. He was suffering from a painful liver complaint which was followed by cerebral sclerosis.

The first Prague Festival of Czech Music was held in the spring of 1904, with Dvořák's works as its centrepiece. A total of 76 choral societies met in the Bohemian capital, 1600 singers took part in the choruses of *St Ludmila* and thousands fêted the composer of the Ninth Symphony and of so many chamber works. Dvořák lay on his sickbed in his apartment in the Korntorgasse, sick also with yearning for Vysoká, where little Pepouschek, his first grandchild, had been his great joy the previous summer.

On 1 May he felt better and joined the family at lunch, but he had barely drunk some soup when he was taken ill again. They put him to bed and called the doctor, who could only confirm that he had died of cerebral apoplexy. Tens of thousands lined the route for his funeral procession, which a few days later passed from the church of St Salvator next to the Charles Bridge through the streets of Prague to the Vyšehrad where, in the last resting place of many great Czechs, Antonín Dvořák was laid in his grave.

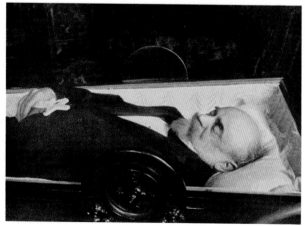

Dvořák laying in state at his funeral in 1904

His Oeuvre and his Standing

Dvořák came slowly to maturity. He was already 40 before the international musical world became aware of him and although he lived into the 20th century his main oeuvre belongs to the 19th – or to be more precise, to the last quarter of that century. In the same period important contemporaries of Dvořák's, also born around 1840, were creating their life's work. They included Brahms, Bizet, Grieg, Fauré, Mussorgsky, Tchaikovsky and Rimsky-Korsakov, a truly variegated assembly with little in common but their position in musical history between two periods, that is, between Wagner, who had pointed the way a generation earlier, and the fin de siècle composers like Strauss, Mahler, Debussy, Schoenberg and Stravinsky, who blazed the trail towards Mussorgsky's 'new shores'.

All creative artists depend on the circumstances, preconditions and conventions of their time, however differently they may develop, and can only be understood in that context and be measured beside their peers, i.e. people of the same generation. Dvořák surpasses them all in the universality of his work.

There is no one to equal him in this respect. One can easily record that others were superior in specific fields: no opera of his can compare with Bizet's *Carmen* or Mussorgsky's *Boris Godunov*, Grieg was a more influential keyboard composer, however modest the contributions of both men may have been; and even in those fields of symphonic and chamber music which were most particularly Dvořák's own, Brahms challenges him for supremacy, however dubious such a comparison may seem. Over and above the fluctuating estimation of his work, the reality of its universality is incontrovertible. Brahms wrote no operas, Mussorgsky no symphonies,

Tchaikovsky no original sacred music. Apart from organ music there is no genre of composition which Dvořák did not provide with fully accomplished works. His oeuvre synthesises not only the instrumental and vocal forms of a whole century but also its stylistic strivings.

Two main tendencies both unsettled and enriched the music of Dvořák's time in the mainstream Germanic world: the antithesis of Wagner's 'endless melody' and Hanslick's aesthetic of 'musically moving forms', and the dialectic of programme and absolute music. A third, on the borders of classical European musical culture, was the coming of young, talented outsiders from the Slav world who, from Chopin and Glinka to Smetana and Mussorgsky, were introducing colours, forms and fables from their hitherto dormant folk music. In Dvořák's work all three streams flow together, not impelled by a towering personality such as that of Beethoven or Wagner (the 'simple Czech music-

Pen and ink portrait of Dvořák at the keyboard by Hugo Boettinger

maker', as Dvořák described himself, would never have compared himself with these masters whom he worshipped from afar), but rather by a disarming naturalness nourished by the very well-spring of creativity.

The Wagnerians could no more adopt Dvořák as their mascot, although he admired Wagner and showed this admiration in both his early and later works, than could the anti-Wagnerian adherents of Brahms, although throughout his life he revered his friend and champion both as a man and an artist. Being a Czech folklorist, Dvořák was regarded as a conservative reactionary by his compatriots, and indeed by contemporary writers on musical politics, who reproached him with betraying Smetana's 'progressive' cause. To this day the conflict between the supporters of Smetana and Dvořák, which reached its most virulent polemical heights in 1912, has been glossed over nationally but not entirely eliminated.

This quarrel seems to the rest of the world a ridiculous domestic Czech squabble. Was there ever a more typical Czech musician than the creator of the Slavonic Dances, the G major Symphony and the Cello Concerto? That Dvořák certainly was – even compared to Smetana, who takes precedence over him both in the field of opera, which was so vital for the Czech national consciousness, and also in intellect and spirituality, in the sense of all that then counted as progressive. Yet regardless of all judgements by his compatriots, which have meanwhile been superseded and completely sidelined, Dvořák must be defended against being labelled a 'Czech music-maker'. This has disparaging and unwarrantably patronising overtones, just as people liked to speak of 'Papa Haydn', as though he were worthy, a bit simple-minded and not to be taken seriously. Dvořák and Haydn shared not only a common ability to think exclusively in terms of sound, as Janáček recognised; they are also united over the passing of more than a century in their universality and pioneering creativity, at least in their national music. If Haydn was the absolute father of the string quartet and the classical symphony, Czech music has Dvořák the music-maker to thank for its first string quartet, first symphony, first instrumental concerto and many others besides.

This achievement, immeasurably great as it was in the development of Czech national music, would not be sufficient to secure for Dvořák a place in world music. Similar pioneering deeds in other emerging musical cultures, such as Glinka's and Moniuszko's operas or Borodin's first Russian symphony, have not been internationally accepted to the same degree as Dvořák's major works. There had to be more to the Slavonic Dances and the

Moravian Duets than just the charm of a refreshingly novel folk-lore element which so delighted contemporaries, if that freshness were to be preserved for over a century and also if those works like the D minor Symphony, which could hardly survive on that charm alone, were to secure recognition. It is in fact Dvořák's high and exceptionally consistent level of compositional skill which determines his standing.

Among the work of almost all great composers, and above all the romantics, one can find puzzlingly inferior by-products, even in the case of geniuses like Beethoven, Schubert or Schumann. Not so with Dvořák. Admittedly his trend was consistently upwards and the gulf between the keyboard studies (which he destroyed or rejected) and his mature works seems vast. This is particularly the case with his operas, the standard of which is of course affected by the extra-musical factors inherent in a complex art-form, most notably the libretto. Where he is fully autonomous and in charge, his mastery is clear from his early years. The Quintet in A minor, written when he was 19, the so-called op 1 (though certainly not his first composition!) is already distinguished by the same exquisite craftsmanship which he lavished on every single work, as he himself acknowledged, and in this respect much less distance seems to separate it from op 105, his last chamber music composition, than 34 years of continuous progress in experience and intellectual maturity might suggest.

When Dvořák was composing at his desk in his Prague apartment – the final phase of a long incubation period – he had a picture of Beethoven on the wall in front of him – almost like an idol, admonishing but unapproachable. He admired and revered Beethoven; Schubert he loved. It may be a coincidence that Dvořák's only important written statement about a fellow composer (he wrote little) was about Schubert and that even this was only printed at second hand and in translation.[85] The affinity between those two great musicians was, however, in no way coincidental. Coming from the same race but different nationalities can have many implications, but in fact Schubert, born in Vienna, had no drop of Viennese blood; on both sides his family was of German-speaking origin but came from Moravia – the same Moravia which put its stamp so decisively on Dvořák's musical idiom. Schubert influenced his Czech colleague more as a symphonist and composer of chamber music than as a song-writer and there are many similarities in their music in those fields: harmonic characteristics – such as a predilection for alternating between major and minor and modulations to the mediant – and thematic structure. In both aspects one's ear is struck by the song-like themes, the prominent cantabile, which one would not single out as the most striking characteristic in the case of other composers whom Dvořák took for his models, such as Beethoven or Brahms.

The description of Dvořák as 'more a melodist than a musical architect'[86] could equally apply to Schubert, as could the observation that exposition of their material was more important than its development, which in the former's case is mostly brief, though certainly not unimportant. By nature a melodist lives by invention. One admires Beethoven for 'fashioning' so much out of so little; with Dvořák one is struck at once by the pronounced, unmistakable pattern of the themes and his seemingly spontaneous and luxuriantly opulent invention. Yet this is misleading. The effect of plasticity and immediacy conveyed by Dvořák's themes is very often the fruit of a long process of thought; his path from initial invention to final form is hardly less complicated than that of Beethoven. He did not leave behind much preparatory material, but in that which survives we can follow very clearly how his ideas evolved, especially in his major works. (How simple and natural the themes of the last two symphonies sound; how completely different and much less substantial they appear in their original form.) Dvořák changed the main theme of the final movement of the *New World* Symphony ten times, the introduction to the adagio five times, and the main theme of the finale of the Eighth Symphony five times, until out of a tune grew the cornerstone of a symphony. He spoke rarely about his compositional technique and even contradicted himself. In 1894, during his last peak period, he said to the composer Foerster, *Invention is everything*, and seven years later to his pupils: *Having a beautiful idea is not so special . . . But developing an idea beautifully and making something great out of it, that is really the hardest, that really is – art.*[87] These statements seem mutually exclusive, but any lack of logic in his artless way of speaking is resolved in his music, where in their final form invention and elaboration merge into an inseparable, interdependent whole. That a composition first strikes one as artless and natural can delude one into overlooking often very complex stages in its creation, which have nothing to do with simplicity.

On the other hand simplification is the badge of the music-maker. It can be said to apply mainly to Dvořák's lack of literary assurance and judgement about opera libretti, but in no way to his absolute music. No naive music-maker sets about selecting, rejecting and refashioning as Dvořák does in his mature chamber works and symphonies. He was not the prolific, un-self-critical writer that his enormous output of more than 150 mostly cyclical works might make him appear. He normally composed at his desk very economically, for only a few hours a day, and if it often seemed amazing that he had put a whole string quartet on paper in a few days, one can be sure that he had gone through a lengthy thought process beforehand.

This comes out most clearly in his absolute music, which lies at the heart of his creative work. This statement is meant relatively, though, and not to the disparagement of his vocal and programme works. On the contrary the best of these, such as the Requiem, the Biblical Songs or the last operas, should be defended against being underestimated abroad, which does not mean shutting one's eyes to the defects of the operas. It hurt him deeply that he did not enjoy nearly the same recognition on the international opera stage as in the concert hall. Occasional, casual remarks – *What do I get out of it if an opera is dramatic! Just the music must be beautiful*[88] – should not be taken as gospel; they are contradicted by the care he lavished on his operas, often rewriting them and revising them at a later date. However, undeniably he lost confidence as soon as he had to deal with a theatrical script. The hallmark of creative originality and perfection which is stamped on his great symphonies and string quartets cannot be ascribed to any of his operas except *Rusalka*, which is increasingly recognised and valued as an artless, late romantic musical fairy tale. All his other operas are handicapped by inadequate libretti. The wealth of superb music he poured out unstintingly in such differing works as the heroically effective *Dimitrij* and the popular, melodic *Jacobin*, should still be strong enough to compensate for their dramaturgical shortcomings – after all, there are enough operas in the repertoire in theatres all over the world with equally poor libretti and worse music – but one overlooks certain weaknesses in good old friends, and in spite of sporadic, though extremely successful performances, *Dimitrij* and *The Jacobin* rank among Dvořák's 'unknown' works outside the Czech Republic.

Another point: someone who is more a melodist than a musical architect must find it most difficult to organise a work of several hours' duration which needs a formally structured blueprint to support it. Not that Dvořák ever composed his operas without planning them, least of all in later life, but he lacked the confidence which being able to model his work within a long-standing tradition would have given him. Such a framework enabled the inexperienced Verdi to write such an accomplished work as *Nabucco* and mediocre musical talents in French opéra-comique to create a wide range of successfully revived works. Nor could

Dvořák call on help from skilled librettists who might have compensated for this lack through their interesting characters, gripping subject matter and accomplished theatrical structure. Dvořák the opera composer was still in the pioneer situation of Smetana and the Russians, who without any tradition behind them had to find their own way between Mozart, Verdi and Wagner towards a national opera, and he shared with them all the inconsistency between musical opulence and lack of an internationally valid theatrical format. The two glorious exceptions, *The Bartered Bride* and *Boris Godunov*, represent the threshold over which only a born opera composer could pass in spite of all obstacles.

Even a purely inspirational literary union, no longer directly throwing up immediate problems of words versus music, became a handicap for Dvořák. Completely voluntarily and against all enticements from his publishers (Simrock would have compensated this world famous composer handsomely for writing new symphonies or string quartets) he decided in his last years to compose tone poems rather than absolute music. Even an apologist like Sychra[89] put Smetana's symphonic poems on a comparatively 'higher level of development', because the older maestro had been successful 'through overcoming the literary element'. In fact Dvořák preferred to cling to his imaginary 'text', though least in the three Slavonic Rhapsodies, whose vague, indefinite 'content' suits them well, and most strongly in the longest of the five tone poems, *The Golden Spinning Wheel*. The composer's adherence to the narrative led him to repeat his motifs, which added so little to the structural strength of the music that even his loving and admiring son-in-law Josef Suk, with the best intentions of rescuing the work, made some radical cuts. This was a significant move, for who would ever have dared to do something of the kind to any of Dvořák's works of absolute music?

31 chamber works, among them 14 string quartets, 50 works for orchestra, including the dramatic overtures, with the nine

symphonies at their centre – this indeed represents a colossal and wide-ranging oeuvre. The number of perfected and unexceptionable works is greater than in the case of most other composers. In quality, of course, the world-famous Ninth Symphony, the Cello Concerto and the American String Quartet stand out, followed at a slight remove by the next best in their genres, according to non-Czech opinion today. But posthumous selection is rigorous and subject to wide fluctuations in judgement as time passes, even in the case of the greatest composers. In Dvořák's case such strokes of genius as the Slavonic Dances or the Slavonic Rhapsodies have slipped away from the concert hall into radio performance and recordings, for the same reason as Smetana's *Vltava*: because they are too 'beautiful' and seem to offer conductors too few challenges and problems to overcome. The apparent sophistication of Dvořák's more complex works has tended to reduce by comparison the value of his simpler ones.

This is very unfair, for the difference between the static, linear structure of the dances or serenades and the thematic development of the symphonies and string quartets is only one of essence, not of quality. In the mature symphonies and chamber music the scherzos strike one as 'Slavonic dances' and the slow movements as artless songs in tertiary form. The simplest pieces are enriched with contrapuntal finesse (such as the bassoon's canon in the seventh Slavonic Dance in C minor) and the technique of varying the themes holds content and form together in the most successful of the symphonic poems like *The Wild Dove*. Whether they are bagatelles, springing spontaneously from a momentary inspiration like most of his piano compositions, or carefully planned major forms, they all bear the unmistakable Dvořák hallmark.

His melodic forms where tune and rhythm are inseparable are the most immediately impressive and here the 'Czech music-maker' is at his most nimble. The fact that he interspersed symphony and sonata (the main form of his chamber music) with dance and introduced the rhythmically characteristic furiant into his symphonies (originally in the scherzo of the Sixth) seems by comparison a superficial momentary excursion into folklore. More significant is that his musical idiom really is a 'language' in the elemental folklore sense and that his tunes are deeply rooted in the intonation of the Czech language. His admirer Janáček raised the stylisation of speech melody (nápěvky) in his operas to the level of a system of composition, while Dvořák worked instinctively and without a system. From his early years he had had an inexhaustible fund of folk tunes in his ears, but however much his themes and melodies are bound up with his conventional musical training in the classics and romantics, in two distinct ways he made them his own: in the insistent lack of upbeats and in the characteristic use of syncopation. Both these features are characteristic of Czech folk music and spring from the intonation of the language. Without exception Czech stresses the first syllable of every word, even if it is a prefix, thereby – in contrast to German – giving its tunes a trochaic and dactylic rhythm devoid of upbeat. The syncopation comes from a particular feature of the Czech language where an unstressed long syllable follows a stressed short one. These characteristics, which are found both in folk songs and in wordless dances, had been directly absorbed and sublimated by Dvořák into his absolute music, where thematic expositions sound as though they were meant to be sung.

It is easy to demonstrate how often Dvořák 'used' models from Czech folklore traditions – and in his American works also from Native American and black folklore. However, nowhere did he do so slavishly, for he had learnt early from Smetana that no serious national music can be created by simply writing down folk tunes. Comparing his raw material and its final form in his scores proves a hundred times that he had mastered the art of truly refining it. His diligence, skill and practical training only served to keep alive the spirit of refreshing and living folklore in forms of highly developed serious music. To this also belongs his preference for pentatonic melody, which forms a completely natural link between the main works of his American period (we can hear pentatonic themes in the *New World* Symphony and the F major String Quartet) and his typically Czech compositions like the Eighth Symphony or the overture *In Nature's Realm*. Tunes in the five-note compass are the universal, elemental property of music, and he had an affinity with elemental music-making, whether he was composing at home or in America.

The same applies to Dvořák's harmonies as to his tunes and rhythms, in that he mostly incorporated characteristics of the folklore of Moravia, which is more striking in this respect than the Bohemian. The so-called 'Moravian modulation' with its changes which break up the classical major – minor into the mixolydian scale or the æolian seventh, had so fascinated Dvořák ever since he worked on the *Moravian Duets* that musicologists like Sychra[90] date a 'radical change' in his style to this moment. Both the Moravian folk song and Dvořák reserve such modulations for dramatic changes in emotional content – another indication of inner harmony. Signs like this should not be overlooked, even if one regards his

Dvořák, entirely a man from the 19th century

harmonic dimensions in general as relatively conventional and committed to the German influence on classical and romantic music. He was not keen on conquering new harmonic terrain. In his later works harmonic variations are intensified and broadened and colour and shading enrich his structures, as in the 'impressionistic' sounds in *Rusalka* or the sequence of triads, E, B-flat, E,

D-flat, B-double flat, G-flat, D-flat, which introduce the largo of the Ninth Symphony with such unprecedented impact – not as a sound in itself, but as an unusually formulated symbol of an unusual psychological landscape. Only the brass and woodwind dispute the musical goings-on – a famous example of his art of orchestration, which has always remained unchallenged. In his music everything can be 'heard', whether in a movement from a string quartet or in a fully scored symphony, because as a practising musician from his early years he understood the capacity of every instrument. Themes, counterpoint and accompanying inner parts are never abstract inventions, but written as it were on the physical instrument in question, so that pure tone-colour effects are rare, one example being the warning voice of the wild dove, symbolised by a harp chirruping over oboe and flute tremuli. More often, virtuosity in the instrumentation serves the particular expression and transparency of the piece. In this respect he follows Wagner in his proximity to the old classical composers, while at the same time foreshadowing the principles of the later Mahler.

Where non-musical problems did not confront him with elements he could not control, Dvořák revealed his gifts as a master of the internal and external proportions of chamber music and symphonies. He was no mystic like Bruckner, no exhibitionist like Tchaikovsky. This late romantic urge to express himself was confined within self-imposed boundaries, where content and form are one. His last symphonies all last for just about forty minutes and the balance between the individual movements is perfect – ten minutes for each of the outer movements, somewhat more for the slow movement and less for the scherzo – as also in the string quartets from the Ninth Quartet on, in the String Sextet (his only piece scored for those forces) and the Cello Concerto. Contemporary Czech critics, taking their cue from the new-German aesthetic of the tone poem, rebuked Dvořák for this formal clarity, based as it was on the German classics and also, naturally, on Brahms, accusing him of using the old forms carelessly and creating 'nothing new'. Such criticism ignores how meticulously Dvořák, experimenting widely and rejecting interim solutions in the manner of Wagner or Liszt, had found his way to creating this form and also with what variety he transformed the classical schema. There is no need to reject the completely innovative 'Dumky' Trio in six movements, for even within traditional formats Dvořák was turning away from formal models. His sonata-variation form with variations in the finale of the Eighth Symphony is as unorthodox as fusing together the themes of all four movements in the finale of the Ninth. How unmistakably the personalities of the last four symphonies derive from the same schema – each one with its own identity and beyond comparison with the others!

'Creating nothing new': such a criticism could make one question Dvořák's entire life's work – not its obvious quality but its position in the historical development of music worldwide. In fact in the perspective of progress there is nothing in Dvořák's work to place him among the trail-blazers of modernism, whose prominent common characteristic during his last years – that is, around 1900 – was to extend harmony beyond the sacred, academic rules of major–minor and in many cases actually to revolt against it. He took absolutely no part in the emancipation of dissonance, to which Mussorgsky, Debussy in *Pelléas et Mélisande* (composed in the 1890s), Schoenberg, Scriabin and even the young Richard Strauss contributed. He did not feel restricted by the dominance of the tonal cadence; to him its laws were inviolable – guarantees of a musical order which simply reflected the order of his world. Discord was to be resolved in concord, the tensions of life were to be overcome through energy and hard work and with God's help. Dvořák's music gives an image of his view of the world – not free from conflict but from the danger of the daemonic – in which art and nature, humanity and metaphysics cannot oppose each other because they all lie in the hands of the Creator, whom he believed in and worshipped unquestioningly. When the musicologist Reinhard Gerlach purported to demonstrate how Dvořák had influenced the most consistently revolutionary element in new music, Arnold Schoenberg,[91] it seemed at first glance astonishing to suggest that any seeds in Dvořák's music could somehow bear fruit in the form of twelve-tone technique; but actually he was referring to the pre-atonal Schoenberg, who in his early D major String Quartet was so influenced by Dvořák's American quartets that he went so far as to quote from them.

Dvořák's image on a Czech stamp celebrating the 50th anniversary of his death in 1954

No, it is completely impossible to fit Dvořák into any perspective of 'progress'. He was no revolutionary, in either harmony or in format, and even the most personal achievement of his music – that of nourishing the European establishment with the vitamins of Czech folk music – does not also enrich the field of historical development. The spring of folklore has been cut off for composers since Bartók and even for those 'post-Webern'. Today the progressive viewpoint, however much it dominates the thinking of 20th-century music historians, is by no means the only one and its legitimacy is validated much more by a variety of preconditions depending on the period – stylistic, social and especially national. Dvořák was entirely a man of the 19th century and what his contemporaries considered progressive or conservative seem today the other way around. Hanslick's tardy reinstatement of him bears witness to this as much as does the revaluation of Verdi's work. For the trend-setting progressives of the day only his *Otello* (mistakenly labelled 'Wagnerian') was worthy to be taken seriously and the younger Verdi of *Il Trovatore* was despised as a composer of hurdy-gurdy music. However, the Verdi renaissance of the 20th century has focused on the early operas, though without underestimating the qualities of his later works.

When determining Dvořák's standing the legitimate yardstick is quality. There is no need to take refuge in irrational spheres and to make judgements of his 'creative personality' in order to establish his quality as a composer. The evidence of his inspiration and high level of professional craftsmanship is incontrovertible and the fact that changes in taste in the course of the 20th century have hardly diminished the popularity of his major works is an indication that they rank as classics. He shares with geniuses from other centuries, like Bach and Mozart, his historical position as a man who embraced the musical universe rather than creating a new one. The discrepancy between his national and international importance does create problems; statistically proven as it is by the huge volume of his works which are living repertoire for Czechs and the narrow selection which has made its mark abroad. There is, however, a move today towards a cautious discovery of the 'unknown Dvořák', though this does not amount to a renaissance such as Janáček has enjoyed since the Second World War.

That he gave to his own people more, much more, than he gave to the world does not diminish Dvořák's greatness. It seems more significant that no other creator of a national music (perhaps with the exception of Chopin, whose much more limited range of compositions was restricted to the keyboard) has grown beyond the principal task set him by his era and environment into international recognition.

Notes

1   Jarmil Burghauser: *Nejen pomníky {Not only memorials} Smetana, Dvořák, Fibich*, Prague 1966

2   Peter Gradenwitz: *Johann Stamitz vol 1 Das Leben {His Life}*, Brno 1936

3   Spitz spelt his name like that but appears in the register as Josef Špic. In any account of Dvořák's life one encounters many such discrepancies, which tell us virtually nothing about ethnic affiliation. At the time German was the main language of officialdom and particularly of the higher professions, so that Czechs used the German spelling of their own names.

4   Recollections of Dvořák's pupil Josef Michl in: *Dvořák ve vzpomínkách a dopisech*, ed Otakar Šourek. *Antonín Dvořák: letters and reminiscences*, 1954. p 19. (future abbrev: LR)

5   Otakar Šourek: *Život a dílo Antonína Dvořáka {Life and work of Antonín Dvořák}*, 4 vols, Prague 1916–1957. vol 1, p 22 (future abbrev. of this definitive monograph: Š)

6   Recollections of Josef Zubatý; LR p 21

7   Letter to Petr Mareš, member of the Interim Theatre orchestra, quoting a conversation with a colleague, Jan Kváča, LR p 25

8   Anna Dušek: Obituary of Antonín Dvořák, LR p 23

9   Přemysl Pražák: *Smetanovy zpěvohry {Smetana's operettas.}*, Prague 1948. vol 1, p 24

10 Its only performance to date was given from the manuscript in Olomouc in 1938

11 According to Adolf Čech, the chorus master at that rehearsal, Š vol 1, p 124

12 Š vol 1, p 121

13 Friedrich Hlaváč: *Anton Dvořák*. In *Nord und Süd*, vol 52, Breslau 1890. p 29

14 Eduard Hanslick: *Concerte, Componisten und Virtuosen der letzten 15 Jahre, 1870–1885 {Concerts, composers and virtuosi of the last 15 years, 1870–1885}*. Berlin 1886. p 245

15 Š vol 1, p 194

16 Eduard Hanslick: *Am Ende des Jahrhunderts {At the end of the century}*. Berlin 1899. p 135

17 On 4 June 1966 at the State Theatre in Brunswick

18   Recollections of Marie Neff; LR p 32

19   The first, rather arbitrary, German translation was by Smetana's friend
     Josef Srb-Debrnov. All 23 duets were published as a cycle in the critical
     Dvořák Collected Edition in 1962 in Prague with the new translation
     by Kurt Honolka, which is more faithful to the original.

20   Dvořák to Brahms, 1877; LR p 33

21   Brahms to Simrock, 1877; LR p 35

22   Max Brod: *Leoš Janáček. Leben und Werk {Leoš Janáček: Life and work}*; LR
     p 75

23   Josef Suk: *Aus meiner Jugend. Wiener Brahms-Erinnerungen {From my youth:
     Memories of Brahms in Vienna}; LR* p 207

24   Brahms to Dvořák, 1878; LR p 38

25   Dvořák to Brahms, 1879; LR p 47

26   According to the German critic Louis Ehlert, whose enthusiastic review
     in the *Berliner National-Zeitung* heralded the triumphal progress of the
     Slavonic Dances

27   Š vol 1, p 118

28   Letter to Simrock, 1888; Š vol 1, p 148

29   Repeated broadcasts of the Hamburg German-language recording in
     Prague, England, Holland, Canada, New Zealand, Austria and
     Switzerland

30   A brilliant performance (conductor: Albert Bittner; director Günther
     Rennert) with Ratko Delorko as Dimitrij, Helga Pilarczyk as Marina
     and Anny Schlemm as Xenia contributed vitally to its unequivocal and
     well-received success. The critic of *Die Welt* sang the praises of 'so much
     strong, inspired music that it is worth getting to know the work at all
     costs', in the Düsseldorf *Mittag* we read: 'It seems strange to us today
     that our opera houses have let this work escape them for so long,
     because *Dimitrij* is the most effective, most beautfiul and most reward-
     ing of all Dvořák's operas.' The Berlin *Tagesspiegel* wrote: 'There is no
     apparent reason for the fate of Antonín Dvořák's opera *Dimitrij*, namely,
     to be consigned to oblivion. The work brims over with invention: tunes
     flow out each moment thrillingly and rhythmically, seem to come
     together into a dramatic dialogue and then spread out once more into a
     oratorio-style design.' The London *Times* wrote of a 'feast of melody' and
     proclaimed that the public had 'received it with the greatest enthusi-
     asm'. *Dimitrij* remained in the repertoire of the Hamburg State Opera
     for four years; however, this extraordinary success of an opera previously
     unknown abroad did not herald a real revival, apart from one production
     in Graz.

31   See for example his letter to Dr Karel Pippich in *Přátelům doma {To
     friends at home}*, Prague-Brno 1941. p 34

32   Libuše Bráfová: *Rieger, Smetana, Dvořák*, Prague 1913. p 111

33   Dvořák to Simrock, 1885; LR p 99

34   Dvořák to Simrock, 1883; LR p 75

35   Š vol 2, p 258

36   Dvořák to his father, 1884; in *Přátelům doma*, op cit p 57

37   Dvořák to Karel Bendl, 1884; ibid p 56

38   Dvořák to his father, 1884; ibid p 57

39   Dvořák to Simrock, 1885; in *Simrock-Jahrbuch {Simrock Diary}* II, p 108

40   Dvořák to Simrock, 1885; ibid p 109

41   Dvořák to Alois Göbl, 1884; in *Přátelům doma,* op cit p 270

42   Dvořák to Bohumil Fidler, 1886; ibid p 88

43   Dvořák to Alois Göbl, 1889; Š vol 2, p 325

44   Dvořák to Simrock, 1890; LR p 140

45   Dvořák to Alois Göbl, 1888; LR p 125

46   The first German-language performance of *The Jacobin* was in 1931 in
     the Town Theatre of Teplice in Northern Bohemia. The conductor Karl
     Elmendorff performed it repeatedly thereafter in Germany and promoted
     it tirelessly. After the Second World War it was performed in 1960 in the
     City Theatre of Wuppertal in Kurt Honolka's new translation.

47   Dvořák to Gustav Eim, 1890; Š vol 2, p 350

48   Š vol 2, p 326

49   From the memoirs of the music critic Ladislav Dolanský; LR p 134

50   From the memoirs of Josef Michl; LR p 149

51   Josef Suk: *Einige Erinnerungen {Some recollections};* LR p 149

52   Ladislav Dolanský: *Aus Dvořáks Schule {From Dvořák's school}*; LR p 151

53   According to Josef Michl; Š vol 3, p 22

54   Dvořák to Josef Hlávka, 1892; Š vol 3, p 95

55   Josef Michl: *Z Dvořákova vyprávnění {From Dvořák's tales}*; In *Hudební
     Revue*, Prague 1914. p 403

56   Š vol 3, p 99

57   Edward Alexander MacDowell in a letter, 1897; Š vol 3, p 125

58   Š vol 3, p 109

59   Dvořák to Simrock, 1893; LR p 188

60   Š vol 3, p 191

61   Dvořák in the *New York Herald*, 12 December 1893

62   Michl: *Z Dvořákova vyprávnění*; LR p 184

63   Š vol 3, p 249

64   Dvořák to Alois Göbl, 1895; Š vol 3, p 249

65   From Josef Kovařík's memoirs; LR p 202

66   Dvořák to Alois Göbl, 1895, in *Přátelům doma*, op cit p 207

67   Karel Weis: *Dvořákovské nápady {Dvořák's ideas}*. In *Národní listy*, Prague,
     1 May 1929

68   Dvořák to Hans Richter, 1896; LR p 214

69   Š vol 3, p 283ff

70   Gustav Mahler to Dvořák, 1898; LR p 225

71   The Czech Philharmonic only became an independent concert orchestra in 1901. From its inception it was closely associated with Dvořák's music.

72   Josef Suk: *Aus meiner Jugend {From my youth}*; LR p 207

73   Interview with Dvořák in the journal *Die Reichswehr*, 1 March 1904; LR p 241

74   Ludwig Speidel in the Vienna *Fremdenblatt*; Š vol 4, p 41

75   The first performance of *Kate and the Devil* in a German theatre was in Bremen in 1909 and then not again until after the First World War. Walter Felsenstein tried to promote a revised version at the Komische Oper in East Berlin. Since 1971 the critical Dvořák Collected Edition has contained a translation by Kurt Honolka which is faithful to the original.

76   LR p 229

77   Dvořák to Alois Göbl, 1900, in *Přátelům doma*, op cit p 227

78   Š vol 4, p 128

79   Š vol 4, p 151

80   Josef Penízek: *Antonín Dvořák als Politiker {Antonín Dvořák as a politician}*; LR p 232

81   Š vol 4, p 185

82   Dvořák to Emil Kozánek, 1902; LR p 237

83   *Armida* was a stranger even to the Czech theatre and only appeared in a new production in 1928 at the Prague National Theatre. Abroad it only appeared on the stage in 1961, when it was performed in Bremen in Kurt Honolka's taut translation. Montserrat Caballé sang the title role.

84   From the memoirs of the virtuoso pianist Josef Faměra; LR p 238

85   Antonín Dvořák: *Franz Schubert.* In co-operation with Henry T Finck. In *The Century Illustrated Monthly Magazine*, New York 1894

86   Antonín Sychra: *Estetika Dvořákovy symfonické tvorby {Aesthetic of Dvořák's symphonic works}*, Prague 1959. p 505

87   Jiří Berkovec: *Antonín Dvořák* Prague-Bratislava 1969. p 279

88   Richard Batka: *Die Musik in Böhmen {Music in Bohemia}*, Berlin 1906. p 76

89   Sychra op cit p 496

90   ibid p 25

91   Reinhard Gerlach: *Dvořáks Einfluss auf den jungen Schönberg {Dvořák's influence on the young Schönberg}*. In *Hudební rozhledy*, Prague 1972. p 84

Chronology

Year	Age	Life
1841		8 September born in Nelahozeves [Mühlhausen]
1847	6	Enters elementary school; first music lessons with his teacher Joseph Spitz
1853	12	Apprenticed to his father as a butcher
1854	13	Further training as a butcher in Zlonice. Promoted to journeyman. Attends the German Middle School, crucial musical training with Anton Liehmann
1856	15	Sent to the Town School in Böhmisch-Kamnitz (Česke Kamenice) to learn German; music lessons with Franz Hanke
1857	16	Goes to Prague to attend the Organ School in the Konviktgasse (Konvitská) and also the German Upper School in the Franciscan Monastery of Maria Schnee
1858	17	Plays the viola in the orchestra at two concerts conducted by Liszt
1859	18	Graduates from the Organ School as a qualified organist. Joins the Komzák light music band as violist
1861	20	Composes op 1, String Quintet in A minor, preceded by many minor compositions
1862	21	Joins the Provisional Theatre Orchestra as violist. Composes First String Quartet in A major
1863	22	Plays in a concert conducted by Richard Wagner
1865	24	First Symphony in C minor
1866	25	Plays as violist in the world premiere of Smetana's *The Bartered Bride*
1870	29	Composes his first opera *Alfred*

Year	History	Culture
1841	In East Africa, Said ibn Sayyid makes Zanzibar his capital.	In Britain, *Punch* magazine founded.
1847	In Yucután Peninsula, War of the Castes. In France, reform banquets held. In Switzerland, Sonderbund War.	Verdi, *Macbeth*. Charlotte Brontë, *Jane Eyre*. Emily Brontë, *Wuthering Heights*.
1853	France annexes New Caledonia. Russia conquers Kazakhstan.	Verdi, *Il Trovatore* and *La Ttraviata*.
1854	In US, Republican Party founded. Pope Piux X declares the dogma of Immaculate Conception of Blessed Virgin Mary to be an article of faith.	Hector Berlioz, *The Childhood of Christ*.
1856	In India, Britain annexes Oudh. Second Anglo-Chinese War (until June 1858).	Liszt, *Hungarian Rhapsodies* Robert Schumann dies
1857	In India, mutiny against the British (until 1858). In Africa, J H Speke 'discovers' source of the Nile.Laying of cable under Atlantic Ocean begun (until 1865).	Charles Baudelaire, *Les Fleurs du Mal*. Gustave Flaubert, *Madame Bovary*. Anthony Trollope, *Barchester Towers*. J F Millet, *The Gleaners*.
1858	Dissolution of English East India Company. At Lourdes, apparition of Virgin Mary.	Jacques Offenbach, *Orpheus in the Underworld*.
1859	Franco-Piedmontese War against Austria. Spanish-Moroccan War (until 1860).	C F Gounod, *Faust*. Wagner, *Tristan und Isolde*. George Eliot, *Adam Bede*.
1861	In US, Abraham Lincoln becomes president (until 1865). In US, Civil War begins (until 1865). In Russia, serfdom abolished.	Dickens, *Great Expectations*. Eliot, *Silas Marner*.
1862	In Prussia, Otto von Bismarck becomes premier.	Verdi, *La Forza del Destino*. Hugo, *Les Misérables*. Turgenev, *Fathers and Sons*.
1863	In US, slavery abolished. In Asia, Cambodia becomes French protectorate.	Berlioz, *The Trojans* (part I). Charles Kingsley, *The Water Babies*.
1865	In US, Abraham Lincoln assassinated. In Belgium, Leopold I dies.	Lewis Carroll, *Alice's Adventures in Wonderland*.
1866	Austro-Prussian War. Austro-Italian War. In Canada, Fenian 'invasion'.	Smetana, *The Bartered Bride*.
1870	Franco-Prussian War. Papal Rome annexed by Italy.	Clément Delibes, *Coppélia*. Dostoevsky, *The House of the Dead*.

1871   30   Composes *King and Charcoal Burner (Kral a Uhlíř)*. Leaves the theatre orchestra. Gives private lessons to earn his living. First public performance of one of his compositions – the song *Meditation (Přemitáni)*

1873   32   17 November, marriage to Anna Čermáková. First significant success as a composer with the cantata *Hymnus*

1874   33   Becomes organist at St Adalbert's church. First performance of one of his operas – the newly composed second version of *King and Charcoal Burner* – at the Provisional Theatre. Completion of a further opera *The Stubborn Lovers (Tvrdé palice)*

1875   34   First awarded the grant of 400 guilders from the Vienna Ministry of Culture. F major Symphony and chamber music composed. First daughter Josefa dies soon after her birth

1876   35   World premiere of the opera *Vanda*. Most of the Moravian Duets and the Piano Concerto in G minor composed

1877   36   Opera *The Cunning Peasant (Šelma sedlák)*, the Symphonic Variations, the *Stabat Mater*, the String Quartet in D minor composed. Brahms brings Dvořák to the attention of Simrock. Deaths of his baby daughter Růžena and baby son Otakar in quick succession

1878   37   Success of the world premiere of *The Cunning Peasant*. First contact with Brahms. First series of Slavonic Dances composed for Simrock. Daughter Otilie born. Third Slavonic Rhapsody composed

1879   38   Brahms comes to Prague. Successes of three Slavonic Dances in London and the Third Slavonic Rhapsody in Berlin and Vienna. Composing the Violin Concerto

1880   39   Daughter Anna born. Travels to Germany. Composes the D major Symphony

1881   40   Daughter Magdalena born. World premiere of the opera *The Stubborn Lovers* in Prague

1882   41   *Dimitrij* given world premiere in the New Czech Theatre and *The Cunning Peasant* at the Dresden State Opera

1883   42   Son Antonín born. Violin Concerto's world premiere with František Ondříček in Prague and soon after performed in Vienna.

1871	At Versailles, William I proclaimed German emperor. In France, Third Republic suppresses Paris Commune and loses Alsace-Lorraine to Germany. In Germany, *Kulturkampf* begins.
1873	In Spain, Amadeo I abdicates; republic proclaimed. In Africa, Ashanti War begins (until 1874). In Asia, Acheh War (until 1903).
1874	In Britain, Benjamin Disraeli becomes prime minister. In Spain, Alfonso XII establishes constitutional monarchy. Britain annexes Fiji islands.

Verdi, *Aïda*.
Carroll, *Through the Looking-Glass*.

Arthur Rimbaud, *A Season in Hell*.
Walter Pater, *Studies in the History of the Renaissance*.
Smetana, *My Fatherland*.
J Strauss, *Die Fledermaus*.
In Paris, first Impressionist exhibition.

1875	In China, Kwang-Su becomes emperor (until 1908). Russo-Japanese agreement over Sakhalin and the Kuriles. In Bosnia and Herzegovina, revolts against Turkish rule.
1876	China declares Korea an independent state. Turkish massacre of Bulgarians. Battle of Little Bighorn; General Custer dies.
1877	Queen Victoria proclaimed Empress of India. Russo-Turkish War. Britain annexes Transvaal. Porfirio Diaz becomes president of Mexico. In Japan, Satsuma rebellion suppressed. Thomas Edison invents gramophone.
1878	Congress of Berlin resolves Balkan crisis. Serbia becomes independent. Britain gains Cyprus. Second Anglo-Afghan War (until 1879).
1879	Germany and Austria-Hungary form Dual Alliance. In Africa, Zulu War. In South Africa, Boers proclaim Transvaal Republic.
1880	In Britain, William Gladstone becomes prime minister. First Boer War (until 1881). Louis Pasteur discovers streptococcus.
1881	In Russia, Alexander II assassinated. In Japan, political parties established. Tunisia becomes French protectorate. In Algeria, revolt against the French. In Sudan, Mahdi Holy War (until 1898). In eastern Europe, Jewish pogroms.
1883	Jewish immigration to Palestine (Rothschild Colonies). Germany acquires southwest Africa. In Chicago, world's first skyscraper built.

Tchaikovsky, First Piano Concerto in B-flat minor. Georges Bizet, *Carmen*. Mark Twain, *The Adventures of Tom Sawyer* (until 1876). Johannes Brahms, *First Symphony*. Wagner, *Siegfried*. First complete performance of Wagner's *The Ring*. Emile Zola, *L'Assommoir*.

Tchaikovsky, *Swan Lake*.

Bruckner, Sixth Symphony. The term 'anti-Semitism' coined by Wilhelm Marr Tchaikovsky, *Eugene Onegin*. Ibsen, *The Doll's House*. Tchaikovsky, *1812 Overture*. Dostoevsky, *The Brothers Karamazov*.

Jacques Offenbach, *The Tales of Hoffmann*. Anatole France, *Le Crime de Sylvestre Bonnard*. Henry James, *Portrait of Lady*. Ibsen, *Ghosts*.

Nietzsche, *Thus Spake Zarathustra*. Robert Louis Stevenson, *Treasure Island*.

Year	Age	Life
1884	43	First journey to conduct his own works in England. *Stabat Mater* greeted with enthusiasm in London. With his earnings buys a country house in Vysoká (Southern Bohemia). In November conducts at the Three Choirs Music Festival and in Berlin
1885	44	Son Otakar born. In London first performance of D minor Symphony, in Birmingham the cantata *The Spectre's Bride (Svatební košile)*. *The Cunning Peasant* performed at the Vienna State Opera. Anti-Czech demonstrations
1886	45	Oratorio *St Ludmila* completed and given world premiere in Leeds in English
1888	47	Meets Tchaikovsky in Prague. Daughter Aloisie born
1889	48	Successful premiere of the opera *The Jacobin (Jacobín)* at the Prague National Theatre. Audience with the Emperor in Vienna. Meets Brahms again
1890	49	G major Symphony first performed. Conducting tour to Moscow and St Petersburg, then return to London. Finishes the Requiem
1891	50	Joins Prague Conservatory as professor of composition. Honorary Doctorates from the Czech University in Prague and Cambridge University, where he conducts his *Stabat Mater* and G major Symphony; thereafter the Requiem in Birmingham
1892	51	Farewell tour through Bohemia before leaving in September for New York, where he remains until spring 1895 as director of the National Conservatory. In October first concert in New York, in November D major Symphony, in Boston the Requiem. Enthusiastic reception everywhere
1893	52	Symphony in E minor *From the New World* completed. Summer holiday in Spillville, Iowa, where he composes the String Quartet in F major and the String Quintet in E-flat major. Guest appearance as conductor at Chicago World Exhibition. Triumphal premiere of the Symphony in E minor in New York
1894	53	Biblical Songs composed in New York. Vacation in Bohemia. Begins the Cello Concerto in New York
1895	54	In April premature return to Prague, from November once more teaching at the Prague Conservatory. Last String Quartets in G major and A-flat major composed

Year	History	Culture
1884	Sino-French War (until 1885). Berlin Conference to mediate European claims in Africa (until 1885). In Mexico, Porfirio Diaz becomes president (until 1911).	Jules Massenet, *Manon*. Mark Twain, *Huckleberry Finn*. Georges Seurat, *Une Baignade, Asnières*.
1885	Belgium's King Leopold II establishes Independent Congo State. Gottlieb Daimler invents prototype of motorcycle.	Zola, *Germinal*. Guy de Maupassant, *Bel Ami*.
1886	In Cuba, slavery abolished. In India, first meeting of National Congress. In Canada, Canadian Pacific Railway completed.	H Rider Haggard, *King Solomon's Mines*. Stevenson, *Dr Jekyll and Mr Hyde*. Rimbaud, *Les Illuminations*.
1888	In Germany, William II becomes emperor (until 1918). In Brazil, slavery abolished.	N Rimsky-Korsakov, *Scheherezade*. Strindberg, *Miss Julie*.
1889	Second Socialist International. Italy invades Somalia and Ethiopia. In Paris, Eiffel Tower completed. Brazil proclaims itself a republic.	Richard Strauss, *Don Juan*. Verdi, *Falstaff*. George Bernard Shaw, *Fabian Essays*.
1890	In Germany, Otto von Bismarck dismissed. In Spain, universal suffrage.	Tchaikovsky, *The Queen of Spades*. Cézanne, *The Cardplayers*. Ibsen, *Hedda Gabler*.
1891	Building of Trans-Siberian railway begins. Shearers' strike in Australia.	Tchaikovsky, *The Nutcracker*. Oscar Wilde, *The Picture of Dorian Gray*. Toulouse-Lautrec, *Le bal du Moulin-Rouge*. Gauguin goes to Tahiti.
1893	Franco-Russian alliance signed. South Africa Company launches Matabele War. France annexes Laos.	Tchaikovsky, *Pathétique*. Wilde, *A Woman of No Importance*.
1894	In France, President Carnot assassinated. Uganda becomes British protectorate. In France, Alfred Dreyfus convicted of treason.	Debussy, *L'Après-midi d'un Faune*. Gabriele d'Annunzio, *Il trionfo della morte*. Kipling, *The Jungle Book*.
1895	In Britain, Lord Salisbury becomes prime minister. Cuban rebellion begins. Japan conquers Taiwan (Formosa). Wilhelm Röntgen invents X-rays.	H G Wells, *The Time Machine*. W B Yeats, *Poems*. Marconi sends message over a mile by wireless. Sigmund Freud publishes first work on psychoanalysis.

Year	Age	Life
1896	55	Cello Concerto premiered under his baton in London and thereafter widely performed. Symphonic Poems *The Water Goblin (Vodník)*, *The Noon Witch (Polednice)*, *The Golden Spinning Wheel (Zlatý kolovrat)* and *The Wild Dove (Holoubek)* composed
1897	56	To Vienna to visit Brahms who is seriously ill. Returns a few weeks later for his funeral
1898	57	Working on the opera *Kate and the Devil (Čert a Káčá)*. Silver wedding, marriage of his daughter Otilie to Josef Suk.
1899	58	World premiere of *Kate and the Devil* at the Prague National Theatre
1900	59	Composes the opera *Rusalka*
1901	60	Brilliant world premiere of *Rusalka* at the Prague National Theatre. Takes the oath as a nominated member of the upper house of the Austrian Parliament in Vienna. Elected director of the Prague Conservatory. Celebrations and festival concerts for his 60th birthday. Dvořák cycle at the National Theatre
1902–03	61–62	Working on the opera *Armida*
1904	62	World premiere of *Armida* only a succès d'estime. Soon after falls ill and dies of cerebral apoplexy on 1 May in his Prague apartment. Funeral on 5 May and burial in the Vyšehrad Cemetery attended by thousands of mourners

Year	History	Culture
1896	Theodore Herzl founds Zionism. First Olympic Games of the modern era held in Athens. Antoine (Henri) Becquerel discovers radioactivity of uranium.	Puccini, *La Bohème*. Thomas Hardy, *Jude the Obscure*. Nobel Prizes established.
1897	In Britain, Queen Victoria celebrates Diamond Jubilee. Britain destroys Benin City. Klondike gold rush (until 1899).	Joseph Conrad, *The Nigger of the Narcissus*. Stefan George, *Das Jahr der Seele*.
1898	Spanish-American War: Spain loses Cuba, Puerto Rico and the Philippines. Britain conquers Sudan.	Henry James, *The Turn of the Screw*. H G Wells, *The War of the Worlds*. Zola, *J'Accuse*.
1899	Second Boer War (until 1902).	Berlioz, *The Taking of Troy*. Elgar, *Enigma Variations*.
1900	First Pan-African Conference. In France, Dreyfus pardoned. Relief of Mafeking.	Puccini, *Tosca*. Conrad, *Lord Jim*.
1901	In Britain, Queen Victoria dies; Edward VII becomes king. In US, William McKinley assassinated; Theodore Roosevelt becomes president.	Strindberg, *The Dance of Death*. Kipling, *Kim*. Thomas Mann, *Buddenbrooks*. Freud, *The Psychopathology of Everyday Life*. Chekhov, *The Three Sisters*.
1902	Peace of Vereeniging ends Boer War. Anglo-Japanese alliance.	Debussy, *Pelléas et Mélisande*. Scott Joplin, *The Entertainer*.
1904	France and Britain sign Entente Cordiale. Russo-Japanese War. Photoelectric cell invented.1904	Puccini, *Madama Butterfly*. G K Chesterton, *The Napoleon of Notting Hill*. Jack London, *The Sea Wolf*. J M Barrie, *Peter Pan*. Chekhov, *The Cherry Orchard*.

Index of Works

The opus numbering is incomplete. Out of about 150 compositions only 115 have opus numbers, which as a result of the contemporary practice of publishers are misleading. Therefore the numbering follows the new 'Thematic Index' compiled by Jarmil Burghauser (see Bibliography), as indicated by the letter 'B'. The dates given indicate firstly when the work was composed, secondly when it was first performed (letter P).

I Vocal Works

OPERAS

Alfred B 16. Text: Theodor Körner. 1870; P 1938

King and Charcoal Burner (Král a Uhlíř) B 21. Text: Bernard J Lobeský (= B Guldener). 1871; P 1929

King and Charcoal Burner (Král a Uhlíř) op 14 – B 21. Text: B Guldener & J Novotný. 1874, 1881, 1887; P 1874

The Stubborn Lovers (Tvrdé palice) op 17 – B 46. Text: Josef Štolba. 1874; P 1881

Vanda. op 25 – B 46. Text: Václav Beneš Šumavský. 1875; P 1876

The Cunning Peasant (Šelma sedlák) op 37 – B 67. Text: Josef Otakar Veselý. 1877; P 1878

Dimitrij op 64 – B 127, 186. Text: Marie Červinková-Riegrová. 1881–1882, revision 1894; P 1882

The Jacobin (Jakobín) op 84 – B 27, 102, 135. Text: Marie Červinková-Riegrová. 1887–1888, revision 1897; P 1889

Kate and the Devil (Čert a Káčá) op 112 – B 201. Text: Adolf Wenig. 1898–1899; P 1899

Rusalka op 114 – B 203. Text: Jaroslav Kvapil. 1900; P 1901

Armida op 115 – B 206. Text: Jarolav Vrchlický. 1902–1903; P 1904

INCIDENTAL MUSIC

Josef Kajetán Tyl op 62 – B 125. Text: F F Šamberk. 1881–1882; P 1882

ORATORIOS, CANTATAS, MASSES

Hymnus 'Heirs of the White Mountain' ('Dědicové Bílé Hory') op 30 – B 27, 102, 135. Text: Vítězslav Hálek. 1872, revisions 1880, 1885; P 1873

Stabat Mater op 58 – B 71. Text: Iacopone da Todi. 1876–1877; P 1880

149th Psalm (Žalm 149) op 49 – B 91, 154. Biblical text. 1879, revision 1887; P 1879

The Spectre's Bride (Svatební košile) op 69 – B 135. Text: Karel Jaromír Erben. 1884; P 1885

St Ludmila (Svatá Ludmila) op 71 – B 144. Text: Jaroslav Vrchlický. 1885–1886; P 1886

Mass in D major (Mše D dur) op 86 – B 135, 175. Liturgical text. 1887, orchestral version 1892; P 1887

Requiem op 89 – B 165. Liturgical text. 1890; P 1891

Te Deum op 103 – B 176. 1892; P 1895

The American Flag op 102 – B 177. Words by J R Drake. 1892–1893; P 1895

Festival Song (Slavostní zpěv) op 113 – B 202. Text: Jaroslav Vrchlický. 1900; P 1900

SONGS FOR SOLO VOICE AND PIANO

Cypresses (Cypřiše) 18 songs with piano B 11. Text: Gustav Pfleger-Moravský. 1865

2 Songs for baritone B 13. Text: Adolf Heyduk. 1865

Songs to texts by Eliška Krásnohorská. 5 songs B 23. 1871

The Orphan, Rosmarine (Sirotek, Rozmarýna) 2 ballads to texts by Karel Jaromir Erben. B 24. 1871

4 Songs on Serbian folk poems op 6 – B 28. 1872

Songs from the Dvůr Králové Manuscript. 6 songs op 7 – B 30. 1872

Evening Songs (Večerní písně). 12 songs op 3, 9, 31 – B 61. Text: Vítězslav Hálek. 1876–1881

3 Modern Greek Songs (Tři novořccké básně), trans. V B Nebeský op 50 – B 84. 1878

Gypsy Melodies (Cigánské melodie). 7 songs to words by Adolf Heyduk op 55 – B 104. 1880

4 Songs on texts by Gustav Pfleger-Moravský op 2 – B 124. 1882

2 Songs on folk verse B 142. 1885

In Folk Tone (V národním tónu). 4 songs op 73 – B 146. 1886

4 Songs on German texts by Ottilie Malybrock-Stieler op 82 – B 157. 1887–1888

Love Songs (Písně milostné). 8 songs on texts by Gustav Pfleger-Moravský op 83 – B 160. 1888

Biblical Songs (Biblické písně). 10 songs from the Old Testament op 99 – B 185. 1894

Lullaby (Ukolébavka) B 194. Text: F L Jelinka. 1895

Song from The smith of Lešetín (Zpěv z Lešetínského kováře) B 204. Text: Svatopluk Čech. 1901

SONGS FOR SOLO VOICE AND ORGAN

Ave Maria op 19b – B 68. 1877

Hymnus ad laudes in festo Sanctae Trinitatis B 82. 1878

Ave Maria Stella op 19b – B 95. 1879

DUETS

Moravian Duets (Moravské dvojzpěvy) for soprano and tenor with piano accompaniment. 4 duets on folk poems op 20 – B 50. 1875

Moravian Duets (Moravské dvojzpěvy) for soprano, contralto and piano. 13 duets on folk poems op 29, 32 – B 60, 62. 1876

Moravian Duets (Moravské dvojzpěvy) for soprano, contralto and piano. 4 duets on folk poems op 38 – B 69. 1877

[Collected edition of all the duets: B 50, 60, 62, 69, 118]

O Sanctissima for contralto, baritone and organ. B 95a. 1879

Child's Song (Dětská píseň) for two unaccompanied voices. B 113. Text: Štěpan Bačkora. 1880

There on our Roof a Swallow Carries (Na tej ňašej střeše) for soprano, contralto and piano on a Moravian folk poem. B 118. 1881

MALE CHORUSES

3 Unaccompanied Choral Songs on folk poems and text by Adolf Heyduk. B 66. 1877

Bouquet of Czech Folksongs (Kytice z českých národních písní). 4 unaccompanied choruses based on folk poems. op 41 – B 72/ 1877

The Song of a Czech (Píseň Čecha) B 73. Text: Fr. Jaroslav Vacek-Kamenický. 1877

From a Bouquet of Slavonic Folksongs (Kyrtice národních písní slovanských). 3 choruses with piano op 43 – B 76. 1877–1878

5 Unaccompanied Choruses on Lithuanian Folk Poems op 27 – B 87.
1878

FEMALE CHORUSES

Moravian Duets (Moravské dvojzpěvy) for 4 unaccompanied voices. 5
choruses. B 107. 1880

MIXED CHORUSES

4 Part-songs for unaccompanied voices op 29 – B 59. Based on folk
poems and texts by Adolf Heyduk. 1876

In Nature's Realm (V přírodě). 5 unaccompanied choruses op 63 – B
126. Text: Vítězslav Hálek. 1882

Hymn of the Czech Peasants (Hymna českého rolníctva). With orchestra op 28 – B 143. Text: Karel Pippich. 1885

II Orchestral Works

SYMPHONIES

1st Symphony in C minor 'The Bells of Zlonice' – 'Zlonické zvony' B
9. 1865; P 1936

2nd Symphony in B-flat major op 4 – B 12. 1865; P 1888

3rd Symphony in E-flat major op 10 – B 34. 1873; P 1874

4th Symphony in D minor op 13 – B 41. 1874; P 1892

5th Symphony in F major op 76 – B 54. 1875; P 1879

6th Symphony in D major op 60 – B 112. 1880; P 1881

7th Symphony in D minor op 70 – B 141. 1884–1885; P 1885

8th Symphony in G major op 88 – B 165. 1889; P 1890

9th Symphony in E minor 'From the New World' – ' Z Nového světa'
op 95 – B 178. 1893; P 1893

SYMPHONIC POEMS, RHAPSODIES

Rhapsody in A minor op 15 – B 44. 1874; P 1894

Slavonic Rhapsodies (Slovanské rapsodie) in D major, G minor and A-flat major op 45 –B 86. 1878; P D major and G minor 1878, A-flat major 1879

The Water Goblin (Vodník). Symphonic poem after the ballad by Karel Jaromír Erben op 109 – B 195. 1896; P 1896

The Noon Day Witch (Polednice). Symphonic poem after the ballad by Karel Jaromir Erben op 108 – B 196. 1896; P 1896

The Golden Spinning Wheel (Zlatý kolovrat). Symphonic poem after the ballad by Karel Jaromir Erben op 109 – B 197. 1896; P 1896

The Wild Dove (Holoubek). Symphonic poem after the ballad by Karel Jaromir Erben op 110 – B 198. 1896; P 1898

Heroic Song (Pise bohatýrská). Symphonic poem op 111 – B 199. 1897; P 1898

CONCERTOS AND CONCERT PIECES

Romance in F minor for violin and orchestra op 11 – B 39. 1877

Concerto in G minor for piano and orchestra op 33 – B 63. 1876; P 1878

Mazurek in E minor for violin and orchestra op 49 – B 90. 1879

Concerto in A minor for violin and orchestra op 53 – B 96. 1879–1880, revision 1882; P 1883

Rondo in G minor for cello and orchestra op 94 – B 181. 1893

Silent Woods (Klid) for cello and orchestra op 68 no 5 – B 182. 1893

Concerto in B minor for cello and orchestra op 104 – B 191. 1894–1895; P 1896

SERENADES, SUITES

Serenade in E major for string orchestra op 22 – B 52. 1875; P 1876

Serenade in D minor for wind instruments, cello and double bass op 44 – B 77. 1878; P 1878

Czech Suite (Česká suita) in D major for chamber orchestra op 39 – B 93. 1 879; P 1879

Suite in A major op 98 – B 190. 1895; P 1910

OVERTURES

Tragic [also Dramatic] Overture (originally the overture to the opera Alfred). B 16. 1870

Overture to Vanda op 25 – B 97. 1879

Overture to Dimitrij *B 127a. 1882*

Overture My Home (Domov můj). From incidental music to Josef Kajetán Tyl op 62 – B 125a. 1882

Hussite Overture (Husitská, dramatická ouvertura) [also Hussite Song] op 67 – B 132. 1883

In Nature's Realm (V přírodě). Concert overture op 91 – B 168. 1892; P 1892

Carnival (Karneval). Concert overture op 92 – B 169. 1891; P 1892

Othello. Concert overture op 93 – B 174. 1891–1892; P 1892

DANCES AND MARCHES

Slavonic Dances (Slovanské tance). First series: C major, E minor, A-flat major, F major, A major, D major, C minor, G minor op 46 – B 83. 1878; P 1878

Festival March (Slavnostní pochod) B 88.1879

Prague Waltzes (Pražské valčíky) B 99. 1879

Polonaise in E-flat major B 100. 1879

Polka in B-flat major 'For the Prague Students' ('Pražským akademikům') B 114. 1880

Slavonic Dances (Slovanské tance). 2nd series: B major, E minor, F major, D-flat major, B-flat minor, B-flat major, C major, A-flat major op 72 – B 147. 1886–1887; P 1887

OTHER ORCHESTRAL

Intermezzos (Meziaktní skladby) for chamber orchestra B 15. 1867

Nocturne in B major for string orchestra op 40 – B 47. 1872; P 1883

Legends in D minor, G major, G minor, C major, A-flat major, C-sharp minor, A major, F major, D major and B-flat minor, op 59 – B 122. 1881

Symphonic Variations op 78 – B 70. 1877; P 1877

Scherzo Capriccioso op 66 – B 131. 1883; P 1884

II Chamber Music

SEXTET

String Sextet in A major op 48 – B 80. 1878; P 1879

QUINTETS

String Quintet in A minor op 1 – B 7. 1861; P 1921

Piano Quintet in A major op 5 – B 28; 1872; P 1872

String Quintet in G major (with double bass) op 77 – B 49. 1875; P 1876

Piano Quintet in A major op 81 – B 155. 1887; P 1888

String Quintet in E-flat major op 97 – B 180. 1893; P 1894

QUARTETS

String Quartet in A major op 2 – B 8. 1862; P 1888

String Quartet in B-flat major. B 17. 1869 (?)

String Quartet in D major. B 18. 1870 (?)

String Quartet in E minor. B 19. 1870 (?)

String Quartet in F minor. B 37. 1873; P 1930

String Quartet in A minor op 12 – B 40. 1873

String Quartet in A minor op 16 – B 45. 1874; P 1875

String Quartet in E major op 80 – B 57. 1876; P 1890

String Quartet in D minor op 34 – B 75. 1877; P 1882

String Quartet in E-flat major op 51 – B 92. 1878–1879. P 1879

String Quartet in C major op 61 – B 121. 1881; P 1882

String Quartet in F major op 96 – B 179. 1893; P 1894

String Quartet in G major op 106 – B 192. 1895; P 1896

String Quartet in A-flat major op 105 – B 195. 1895; P 1897

String Quartet 'Cypřiše' – 'Cypresses' (12 pieces). B 152. 1887

Piano Quartet in D major op 23 – B 53. 1875; P 1880

Piano Quartet in E-flat major op 87 – B 162. 1889. P 1890

Bagatelles (Malíčkosti) for two violins, cello and harmonium op 47 – B 79. 1878; P 1879

TRIOS

Piano Trio in B-flat major op 21 – B 51. 1875; P 1877

Piano Trio in G minor op 26 – B 56. 1876; P 1879

Piano Trio in F minor op 65 – B 130. 1883; P 1883

Terzetto in C major for two violins and cello op 74 – B 148. 1887; P 1887

Miniatures (Drobnosti) for two violins and cello op 75a – B 149. 1887; P 1938

Gavotte for three violins. B 164. 1890

Dumky. Trio for piano, violin and cello op 90 – B 166. 1890–1891; P 1891

VIOLIN AND PIANO

Romance in F minor op 11 – B 38. 1873–1877

Nocturne in B major op 40 – B 48. 1875–1883

Capriccio. B 81. 1878

Mazurek op 49 – B 89. 1879

Sonata in F major op 57 – B 106. 1880

Ballad in D minor op 15 no 1 – B 139. 1884

Romantic Pieces (Romantické kusy). 4 pieces op 75 – B 150. 1887; P 1887

Sonatina in G major op 100 – B 183. 1893

CELLO AND PIANO

Concerto in A major. B 10. 1865

Polonaise in A major. B 94. 1879. P 1879

Rondo in G minor op 94 – B 171. 1891; P 1892

Silent Woods (Klid) op 68 no 5 – B 173. 1891

PIANO FOR TWO HANDS

2 Minuets op 18 – B 58. 1876

Dumka op 35 – B 64. 1876

Theme with variations op 36 – B 65. 1876

Scottish Dances (Škotské tance) op 41 – B 74. 1877

Furiants in D major and F major op 42 – B 85. 1878

Silhouettes. 12 pieces op 8 – B 98. 1879

Waltzes in A major, A minor, E major, D-flat major, B-flat major, F major, D minor and E-flat major op 54 – B 101. 1880

Eclogues in F major, D major, G major and E major op 56 – B 103. 1880

Album Leaves (Listky do památníku) 1–4. B 109. 1880

Piano pieces (Impromptu, Intermezzo, Gigue, Eclogue, Allegro molto, Tempo di marcia) op 52 – B 110. 1880

Mazurkas in A-flat major, C major, B-flat major, D minor, F major and B minor op 56 – B 111. 1880

Impromptu in D minor. B 129. 1883

Dumka and Furiant op 12 – B 136, 137. 1884

Humoresque in F-sharp major. B 138. 1884+

Two Little Pearls (Dvě perličky). In a ring: grandpa dances with grandma. B 156. 1887

Poetic Tone Pictures (Poetické nálady). Nocturnal path (Noční cestou); Toying (Žertem); At the Old Castle (Na starém hradě); Spring Song (Jarni); Peasant Ballad (Selská balada); Reverie (Vzpomináni); Furiant; Goblins' Dance (Rej skřitků); Serenade; Bacchanal (Bakchanale); Tittle-Tattle (Na táčkách); By the Tumulus (U mohyly); On the Holy Mountain (Na svaté hoře) op 85 – B 161. 1889

Suite in A major op 98 – B 185. 1894

Humoresques in E minor, B major, A-flat major, F major, A minor, B major, G-flat major and B-flat minor op 101 – B 187. 1894

Berceuse and Capriccio B 188. 1894

PIANO FOR FOUR HANDS

Slavonic Dances (Slovanské tance). 1st series (see p144) op 46 – B 78. 1878

Legends (see p145) op 59 – B 117. 1880–1881

From the Bohemian Forest (Ze Šumavy). 6 character pieces (At Spinning Time (Na přástkách); By the Black Lake (U černého jezera); Witches' Sabbath (Noc filipojakubská); On the Watch (Na čekání); Silent Woods (Klid); In Stormy Times (Z bouřlivých dob) op 68 – B 133. 1884

Slavonic Dances (Slovanské tance). 2nd series (see p145) op 72 – B 145. 1886

Bibliography

Square brackets are used for translations of the titles of works of which there is no known English version
Abbreviations: C/Mc = Current Musicology, ML = Music and Letters, MQ = The Musical Quarterly, MR = The Music Review, MT = The Musical Times, PMA = Proceedings of the Musical Association

CATALOGUES

O Šourek: *Dvořák Werke: ein vollständiges Verzeichnis*, [A complete index], Berlin 1917.

J Burghauser: *Antonín Dvořák: thematický katalog, bibliografie, přehled života a dila* [Thematic catalogue, bibliography, survey of life and work], Prague 1960

SOURCE MATERIAL

R Newmarch: *The Letters of Dvořák to Hans Richter*, MT, lxxiii 1932, pp 605, 698, 795

O Šourek: *Dvořák ve vzpomínkách a dopisech*, Prague 1938/9, 1951. Eng trans: 'Antonín Dvořák: Letters and Reminiscences', 1954

Hořejš: *Antonín Dvořák: the Composer's Life and Work in Pictures*, Prague 1955

J Clapham: *Dvořák and the Philharmonic Society*, ML xxxix,1958, p 123

—*Dvořák's Visit to Russia*, MQ li 1965, p 493

—*Dvořák's Relations with Brahms and Hanslick*, MQ lvii 1971, p 241

—*Dvořák's Unknown Letters on his Symphonic Poems,* ML lvi 1975, p 277

E Herzog: *Antonín Dvořák v obrazech* [Dvořák in Pictures], Prague 1966

K Honolka: *Antonín Dvořák in Selbstzeugnissen und Bilddokumenten,* Reinbek 1974

MEMOIRS

J M Thurber: *Dvořák as I knew him*, Étude xxxvii 1919, p 693

R Evans: *Dvořák at Spillville*, 'The Palimpsest' xi Iowa City 1930, p 113

E Hanslick: *Concerte, Componisten und Virtuosen,* Vienna 1879, Berlin 1886.

Eng trans: 'Anton Dvořák', MR i/9 New York 1879, p 141

J Bennett: *The Music of Anton Dvořák,* MT xxii 1881, pp 165, 236

W H Hadow: *Antonín Dvořák*, in 'Studies in Modern Music', 2nd series, London 1895

F J Sawyer: *The Tendencies of Modern Harmony as exemplified in the Works of Dvořák and Grieg*, PMA xxii 1895/6, p 53

O Šourek: *Antonín Dvořák*, Prague 1929. Eng trans 1952

O Šourek & P Stefan: *Dvořák: Leben und Werk,* Vienna 1935. Eng trans 'Anton Dvořák', 1941

V Fischl (ed): *Antonín Dvořák: his Achievement,* London 1942

A Robertson: *Dvořák*, London 1945, rev 1974

J Burghauser: *Antonín Dvořák,* Prague 1966. Eng trans 1967

J Clapham: *Antonín Dvořák: Musician and Craftsman*, London 1966

SPECIFIC WORKS

O Šourek: *Dvořákovy symfonie*, Prague 1922. Eng trans in 'The Orchestral Works of Antonín Dvořák', 1956

—*Dvořákovy skladby komorní,* Prague 1943. Eng trans (abridged), 'The Chamber Music of Antonín Dvořák', 1956

— *Dvořákovy skladby orchestralní*, Prague 1944-6. Eng trans (abridged) 'The Orchestral Works of Antonín Dvořák', 1956

D Tovey: *Essays in Musical Analysis*, London 1935-9/1972

J Clapham: *The Evolution of Dvořák's Symphony 'From the New World'*, MQ xliv 1958, p 167

—*Dvořák's Cello Concerto, a Masterpiece in the Making*, MR xl 1979, p 123

—*Indian Influence on Dvořák's American Chamber Music*, Musica cameralis Brno VI 1971, p 174

J Harrison: *Antonín Dvořák,* in 'The Symphony', ed R Simpson, Harmondsworth 1966

R Layton: *Dvořák: Symphonies and Concertos*, London 1978

D Beveridge: *Sophisticated Primitivism: the Significance of Pentatonicism in Dvořák's 'American' Quartet*, C\Mc 1977 no 24, p 25

J Smaczny: *Armida – Dvor'ák's Wrong Turning?. Zpráva iii/5, London 1977, p 10

M Černý: *Zum Wort-Ton-Problem im Vokalwerk Antonín Dvořáks*, in 'Music and Word', Brno IV 1969, p 139

Testimonials

JOHANNES BRAHMS

The fellow has more ideas than all of us. Anybody else could cobble together main themes out of what he throws away.

BEDŘICH SMETANA

There must be something inside such a powerful head! And in the interests of the further development of our music I am happy to have such an excellent rival . . . Everyone should compose to the best of his ability and value his colleague's work as highly as he wants to be valued by others – only in this way shall we advance and raise the level of our art.

GEORGE BERNARD SHAW

The symphony [no 8 in G major] almost reaches the level of Rossini's overtures and would make excellent promenade music for summer parties in the country.

LEOŠ JANÁČEK

I am convinced that in Antonín Dvořák we have the only national Czech composer.

. . . I am convinced that Mr Dvořák's scores are masterpieces of counterpoint. As a rule he is not content to create a clear, interesting harmonic basis with a single motif: two, three or even up to five striking themes appear simultaneously... A musician can come to love Dvořák's scores. What is most important, Dvořák does not continue a figure in one part to excess; you have hardly made its acquaintance when the second one is beckoning to you with a friendly gesture. You are in a state of continual, pleasurable excitement . . .

You know the feeling when someone takes the words out of your mouth before you can say them? That's how I always feel in Dvořák's company. To me the man and his work are interchangeable. He took his melodies from my heart.

ZDENĚK NEJEDLÝ

If I were to give my opinion of Dvořák, I could today [1913] say no more than that he does not interest me. To me this is a chapter in Czech music which is dead and gone and in which there is little to engage an enquiring and creative spirit. To me Dvořák is rather like Mendelssohn in German music, though of course in a reduced, Czech version... He presents a massive obstacle, which any young Czech musician must remove from his path if he is to make progress.

VÁCLAV TALICH

He is the complete master of the technical craft of his era and even goes beyond it (I am thinking of Brahms), but he complements it with the spirit of his native land and in my opinion Antonín Dvořák made this contribution to the course of the world.
Jean Sibelius

Only rarely is the outward expression of an artist in such perfect harmony with his art as in the case of this great Czech artist, in whose works the purely human and the artistic side form a harmonic whole which I shall never forget.

Dvořák was one of those people who showed me the path which an artist and composer should follow, perhaps because he gave such forthright expression to his people and his Czech origins and because in this respect there was something which I myself wanted to express. To me Dvořák's personality seems imbued with a precious quality of kindness, humanity and sanity. If anyone expressed a healthy and happy relationship to life, it was he . . . Music should always be joyful, even when it is tragic. He is a happy man who leaves such a legacy behind him.

About the Author

Dr Kurt Honolka, musical author and critic, was born in 1913 in Leitmeritz (Bohemia) and studied at the German University in Prague. He worked from 1949 to 1963 as a journalist on the *Stuttgarter Nachrichten* and since then as music and theatre critic for that paper and for other German and foreign publications and radio stations.

Publications: *Weltgeschichte der Musik (World history of music), Geschichte der Russischen Musik (History of Russian music), Kulturgeschichte des Librettos (A cultural history of the libretto), Das vielstimmige Jahrhundert – Musik in unserer Zeit (The polyglot century – Music in our time), Opernführer (Opera Guide).*

As a translator and reviser of operas, songs and choral works, particularly by Smetana, Janáček and Dvořák, he was a committed spokesman for classical and contemporary Slav music. He died in 1988.

Picture Sources

All photographs and illustrations courtesy the
Lebrecht Picture Library, London.

Index

Chopin, Frédéric, 3, 90, 114, 127

classicism, 4, 25, 92

Clementi, Muzio, 58

Coleridge-Taylor, S, 89

Cologne, 37, 49

Comenius, Johann Amos, 6

Communism, 5

Corri, P A, 58

Counter-Reformation, 5

Cramer, J B, 58

Croydon, 89

Czech impressionism, 107

Czech language, 6–8, 26, 55, 108, 122

Czech Philharmonic Orchestra, 98

Dalibor, 22, 34

Damrosch, Leopold, 82, 84

Dance, W, 58

de la Motte-Fouqué, Friedrich Heinrich Karl, 105

Debussy, Claude, 107, 113; *Pelléas et Mélisande*, 125

Des Knaben Wunderhorn, 96

Die Reichswehr, 102

Dobrovský, Josef, 8

Dover, 60

Drake, Joseph Rodman, 74

Dresden, 37, 49, 57, 72

dumka, 35, 48, 69

Dušek, Anna, 21

Dušek, Václav, 17

Dvořák , Anna (née Čermáková), 21, 22, 32, 57, 78

Dvořák , Anna (née Zdeňková), 13; death, 50

Dvořák , Antonín: reputation, 1–3; birth and childhood, 11–13; musical training, 13–15; early compositions, 15, 18, 19, 24–5, 26–9; move to Prague, 15–21; earnings, 19–20, 32, 44, 62–3, 77, 98; appearance, 20; lifestyle, 21, 80, 98–9; love affair, 21–2, 24, 29; marriage, 22, 32; first success, 28, 29–31; children's deaths, 32, 39; walking tour with Janáček, 32; receives grant, 32–4, 41; finds own identity, 34; Catholicism, 39, 43, 54–5, 100, 110, 126; friendship with Brahms, 41–3, 55, 94, 99–100, 114; international recognition, 42, 57, 72, 97, 127; interest in trains, 45, 81; Slavonic periods, 46, 68; in England, 57–63, 66, 72, 75, 99; buys own home, 62; delight in composing, 67; arguments with Simrock, 66, 67–8; friendship with Tchaikovsky and visit to Russia, 72; honoured, 75, 98, 101, 108–9; head of School of Composition, 76; teaching, 76–7, 111; in America, 79–92; agoraphobia, 81; interest in ships, 81; popularity in America, 84, 98; happiness, 93–4; silver wedding, 101; on opera, 102, 111; appointed to second house of Austrian Parliament, 108; director of Prague Conservatory, 108–9; 60th birthday, 109; taken ill, 111–12; death, 112; universality, 113, 115; compositional skill, 116; compositional habits, 117–19

WORKS: First Symphony in C minor *The Bells of Zlonice*, 14, 24–5; First Cello Concerto, 24; *Alfred*, 26; *Cypresses*, 24, 68; String Quartets in D major, B-flat major and C minor, 25; *The Lark*, 31; String Quintet in A minor op 1, 18, 116; String Quartet in A major op 2, 18; *Evening Songs*, 39; Second Symphony in B-flat major op 4, 24; Piano Quintet in A major op 5, 30, 68; Songs from the Dvůr Králové manuscript, 27–8; Third Symphony in E-flat major op 10, 30, 32; String Quartet in F minor, 30; String Quartet in A minor op 12, 30–1; Fourth Symphony in D minor op 13, 34, 44; *King and Charcoal Burner* op 14, 27, 29, 68; Rhapsody in A minor op 15, 31, 34; String Quartet in A minor op 16, 34; *The Stubborn Lovers* op 17, 35, 109; *Moravian Duets* op 20, 38, 44, 45, 116, 123; Piano Trio in B-flat major op 21, 35; String Serenade op 22, 35; Piano Quartet in D major op 23, 35; *Vanda* op 25, 36, 51; Piano Trio in G minor op 26, 35; *Hymnus* op 30, 28, 29; Piano

Note on the Czech Language

All Czech words without exception have their stress on the first syllable. An acute accent over a vowel (eg 'á') indicates length, not stress.

Pronunciation of accented letters:
č = ch as in church,
ě = ye as in yes,
ň = n-ye,
š = sh,
ž = 'je' (French for 'I'),
ř = combines r and 'je'.
The name Dvořák is common in Bohemia and Moravia and means
'man from a farm'.

LIFE & TIMES FROM HAUS

Churchill
by Sebastian Haffner
'One of the most brilliant things of
any length ever written about
Churchill.' *TLS*
1-904341-07-1 (pb) £8.99
1-904341-06-3 (hb) £12.99

Dietrich
by Malene Skaerved
'It is probably the best book ever on
Marlene.' C. Downes
1-904341-13-6 (pb) £8.99
1-904341-12-8 (hb) £12.99

Beethoven
by Martin Geck
'...this little gem is a truly handy ref-
erence.' *Musical Opinion*
1-904341-00-4 (pb) £8.99
1-904341-03-9 (hb) £12.99

Prokofiev
by Thomas Schipperges
'beautifully made, ... well-produced
photo-graphs, ... with useful historical nuggets.' *The Guardian*
1-904341-32-2 (pb) £8.99
1-904341-34-9 (hb) £12.99

Curie
by Sarah Dry
'...this book could hardly be bettered' *New Scientist*
selected as **Outstanding Academic Title**
by *Choice*
1-904341-29-2 (pb) £8.99

Einstein
by Peter D Smith
'Concise, complete, well-produced and lively throughout, ... a bargain at the price.' *New Scientist*
1-904341-15-2 (pb) £8.99
1-904341-14-4 (hb) £12.99

Casement
by Angus Mitchell
'hot topic' *The Irish Times*
1-904341-41-1 (pb) £8.99

Britten
by David Matthews
'I have read them all - but none with as much enjoyment as this.' *Literary Review*
1-904341-21-7 (pb) £8.99
1-904341-39-X (hb) £12.99

De Gaulle
by Julian Jackson
'this concise and distinguished
book' Andrew Roberts *Sunday
Telegraph*
1-904341-44-6 (pb) £8.99

Orwell
by Scott Lucas
'short but controversial assessment
... is sure to raise a few eyebrows'
Sunday Tasmanian
1-904341-33-0 (pb) £8.99

Bach
by Martin Geck
'The production values of the book
are exquisite, too.'
The Guardian
1-904341-16-0 (pb) £8.99
1-904341-35-7 (hb) £12.99

Kafka
by Klaus Wagenbach
'One of the most useful books about
Kafka ever published' *Frankfurter
Allgemeine Zeitung*
1-904341-02 -0 (PB) £8.99
1-904341-01-2 (hb) £12.99

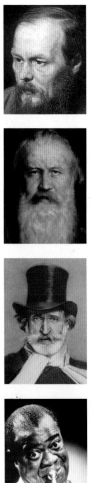

Dostoevsky
by Richard Freeborn
'... wonderful ... a learned guide' *The Sunday Times*
1-904341-27-6 (pb) £8.99

Brahms
by Hans Neunzig
'readable, comprehensive and attractively priced'
The Irish Times
1-904341-17-9 (pb) £8.99

Verdi
by Barbara Meier
'These handy volumes fill a gap in the market ... admirably.' *Classic fM*
1-904341-21-7 (pb) £8.99
1-904341-39-X (hb) L12.99

Armstrong
by David Bradbury
'generously illustrated ... a fine and well-researched introduction' George Melly *Daily Mail*
1-904341-46-2 (pb) £8.99
1-904341-47-0 (hb) £12.99